PRAISE FOR ~~F~~

"Amy Banks and Issac Kna[...] [...]ries of two families, whose lives i[...] [...] 1979 and unfold a series of events that r[...] [...] lives forever. Blended together, much like a catastrophic earthquake, they spend the next three decades trying to find anything salvageable from their former lives. *Fighting Time* is not just a book about the injustice of a wrongful conviction, but a love story of the capacity of human beings to find power in the pain and healing in the harm."

–Jennifer Thompson, co-author of the best selling *Picking Cotton*

"*Fighting Time* is a brave and necessary book. It is a book that pushes the reader beyond thin and familiar abstractions about social justice and systemic oppression. In this book, Dr. Amy Banks and Mr. Isaac Knapper put flesh and bone and spirit onto institutional practices and social behaviors designed to lock inequalities in place, thus perpetuating the chronic disconnections that corrode the human spirit.

"There are some books that make it impossible to 'not know.' *Fighting Time* is such a book. One enters into the book and is confronted with questions that can only be answered by radical engagement with the life of those we call Other and by confronting the illusions and denials that comprise what is called Self. The reward is a renewed claim on human dignity, a strengthened commitment to social justice, and perhaps a revisioning of human possibility."

–Maureen Walker PhD, author of *When Getting Along is Not Enough: Reconstructing Race in Our Lives and Relationships*

"Racial inequalities permeate every aspect of our culture and *Fighting Time* reminds us how those inequities affect our perspectives, experiences, and life outcomes. It reflects how little has changed when it comes to the treatment of our most underserved and vulnerable populations and how grief and loss can bring divided communities and people together. *Fighting Time* reminds the reader of the importance of seeing past zip code, skin color, education and age, factors our unjust systems are created to reward or punish.... *Fighting Time* will inspire its readers to build a movement of connection, forgiveness and change."

—Inderjit (Vicky) Basra, President/CEO of Delores Barr Weaver Policy Center, Jacksonville, FL

"This is an incredible story, a memoir of trauma in two voices, each wounded, each courageous, and each inviting us into a story of healing and recovery. This book is a deep dive into the worlds of mental health and social justice that demonstrates their inseparable connection."

—Anne Hallward MD, Host of Safe Space Radio

"*Fighting Time* is a profound, sometimes shocking but beautifully poignant story about two teens on the cusp of their lives, who are tragically affected by a random violent act. Amy Banks and Isaac Knapper are brutally honest and boldly vulnerable as they describe the far-reaching ripple effects of their trauma, showing us how a singular event can profoundly change the trajectory of one's life. Decades later, after an unusual turn of events, this unlikely pair is brought together by a force larger than them, teaching us all how resilience, persistence, sheer will, and a loving connection can help transform us, heal our pain, and find lasting peace from the unspeakable... They have joined forces to prove, beyond a shadow of a doubt, that truth, love, and the tenacity of the human spirit conquers all."

—Frank G. Anderson, MD, author of *Transcending Trauma: Healing Complex PTSD with Internal Family Systems Therapy*

"This book is a must-read for anyone interested in the purpose and utility of our carceral systems, exploring the cascading effects of trauma on behavior, and anyone doing the work of critically investigating systems to reimagine safety, justice, [human] connection, reconciliation, and the wholeness of the human condition."

—Kenitra Brown, Director of Engagement & Staff Attorney, Deason Criminal Justice Reform Center, SMU Dedman School of Law, Founding Board Member Power in Action-Dallas

FIGHTING TIME

Amy Banks and Isaac Knapper

Pact Press

Published by Pact Press
An imprint of
Regal House Publishing, LLC
Raleigh, NC 27612
All rights reserved

https://pactpress.com

Printed in the United States of America

ISBN -13 (paperback): 9781646031672
ISBN -13 (epub): 9781646031689
Library of Congress Control Number: 2020951939

Interior design by Lafayette & Greene
Cover design by C.B. Royal
Cover images © by sutadimages/Shutterstock

Regal House Publishing, LLC
https://regalhousepublishing.com

Printed in the United States of America

Amy—to my parents, Dr. Ronald and Helena Banks

Isaac—to all my friends and comrades at Angola State Penitentiary. Stay strong, my brothers

"The hottest places in hell are reserved for those who, in a period of moral crisis, maintain their neutrality."

- Dante quote, found in the wallet of Dr. Ronald Banks at the time of his murder.

1

Goodbye

Amy Banks

The day my father was murdered unfolded like most days in my seventeenth year. I woke up bleary-eyed around 6:45, poured myself a bowl of Honeycomb cereal with milk, and retreated to my bedroom to eat in solitude, blocking out the irritating sounds of my parents and younger sister preparing for their day. When my brother moved to a dorm at the University of Maine in the fall of 1978, I inherited his basement bedroom and that room became my launching pad for independence. With it came a host of teenage perks: bunk beds, an old pool table, a cheap stereo, a couch, even a toilet and sink in the laundry room. On the day he moved out, I hung fifty of my favorite baseball hats on the wall closest to my bed, like a dog marking his territory. In this new space I pretended I'd already escaped the chaos of my family.

The week my father was murdered was big for me even before he was killed. Gigantic, really, in a way that only happens in the egocentric world of a carefree teenager. At the time, basketball sat squarely at the center of my life. My top priority wasn't family, or school, or boyfriend, or parties. It was taking two hundred jump shots a day, rain or shine, sleet or snow, on a small basketball hoop in my neighbor's backyard. My discipline was about to pay off. Three days earlier, our local newspaper had sent a photographer to our house to snap a headshot of me for the weekend edition where the annual All-State basketball selections would be announced. Making the team had been one of my individual goals for the season, and though the photographer gave me no assurance that I had been selected, it seemed like a lot of extra work if I hadn't been chosen. Still, I couldn't be sure until I saw my face on the front page of the sports section that weekend. I thought of nothing else as the week slowly ticked by.

My family is not demonstratively affectionate. Both my parents were born and raised in Camden, Maine, back when it was still a lobster town. They were raised in the old New England traditions of stoicism and practicality. When I was younger, my father would leave for work while my siblings and I were still eating breakfast. He would give each of us a quick peck on the top of our head. Often, when he got to me, he would start with a kiss and then give me a playful, juicy raspberry on the neck or cheek. I hated it. It felt like proof that he didn't like me as much as my other siblings, a belief my brother regularly encouraged.

After my two older siblings, Kate and Phil, left home to go to college, my father's comings and goings were background noise. Occasionally I might hear "See you later" drift down the stairwell as the front door closed. On the day he was murdered I was too involved in my own world to remember when and where he was going. Truth be told, I didn't really care. But that morning was different—he came down to say goodbye face to face and to make a plan before flying to New Orleans for the Organization of American Histories (OAH) annual conference.

My dad had been an accomplished athlete himself and everything positive between us revolved around our mutual love of sports. Even now, decades later, my most cherished possessions include original newspaper clippings from the *Camden Herald* showing him sliding safely into third base under a tag and jumping over a group of sweaty teenage boys to grab a rebound. I still keep his flat, worn baseball glove tucked away in a large wooden box that holds all I have left of him, each item precious and intimate—the plaque he won in a middle-school spelling bee, his wallet, pipe, and comb, and the wide, brown tie he wore the night he was shot. Each item carries his scent, his DNA. The box also contains evidence of his murder. Laminated front-page newspaper stories of the killing and piles of condolence letters from friends, colleagues, old teachers, students, and even complete strangers who were moved to write to my family after reading about our tragedy in the paper.

When he came down the stairs that morning, I was packing my gym bag for softball practice after school. I paused momentarily and listened. He would be gone for the entire weekend and wanted to figure out how he could learn the results of the All-State selection as soon as they were published. Together we came up with a plan that I would drive to the *Bangor Daily News* headquarters around midnight on Friday to get the first copies of the weekend edition hot off the press. He would then call me from New Orleans to hear what team I had made. This was long before cell phones, and our plan required a concentrated effort from both of us to get to a phone at the appointed time. As he lowered his head under the doorway on his way out, he wished me luck. Those were the last words he shared with me, the planned celebration aborted by his death. At the designated time on Friday night, my father was in a Louisiana morgue, and I entered a deep freeze from which I am just now emerging.

When the newspaper came out on Saturday, the headshot taken earlier in the week was part of the annual All-State selection spread. I had made the cut. But in the very same edition, the front-page headlines featured the news of my father's shocking murder. This tragic coincidence created an overwhelming emotional stimulus that wired my father's death and my success into a haunting neural network—a template of fear that has followed me throughout my life. When things are really good or success is just around the corner, I can tolerate it only so long, because I know deep in my bones that it will be followed by some unspeakable tragedy.

Life's unpredictability and the regular losses of life provided the intermittent reinforcement needed to lock this network in place. A virtual Möbius strip of perpetual fear and pain—father, death, murder, my success, murder, death, father. Did I blame myself for my father's murder? Not consciously, but somewhere deep in my subconscious—where I couldn't make sense of a world that killed fathers on business trips—I knew that had I been more attentive that morning, less critical of the clothes my dad wore, less preoccupied with my All-State selection, he would be alive today.

Brewer, Maine
7:45 a.m.
April 12, 1979

On the day he died, my father walked out of our house looking professorial in his new trench coat and tortoise-shell glasses, a black briefcase at his side. My mother and eight-year-old sister, Nancy, were sitting in our maroon Chevy Impala waiting for him. He maneuvered his long limbs into the driver's seat and adjusted the mirrors for the twenty-minute trip to the airport. Just like that he was gone. Forever. One of the most difficult aspects of a sudden, violent death is that there is no time to brace yourself for the emotional tsunami to come. No time to board up the doors and tape the windows; no time to find higher ground to watch the events unfold. One minute you're mindlessly moving through your day, and the next you're trying desperately to keep your head above water, the emotional eddies swirling around your feet.

As my father headed to New Orleans, I spent another day oblivious to the reality that my comfortable life was about to be turned upside down. My boyfriend, Doug, picked me up for school. I went to my Thursday classes, practiced softball after school, and got a haircut that was way too short. April 12, 1979, was shaping up to be one of those days that simply disappear into the deepest recesses of your brain, never to be recalled.

My mother was anxious at baseline, but when my father traveled her tension and fear expanded, filling the house with an electric buzz. I'm convinced that her pervasive distrust of the world stemmed from a childhood growing up in the '30s and '40s in a coastal town in Maine with a mother who worked outside the home by choice rather than need. Her mother's nickname was Dot (we kids knew her as Nana), which was the perfect label for a diminutive woman who was as round as she was tall. She was also cold, stern, and distant. She lacked a basic sense of nurturance as evidenced by her regularly whacking her cocker spaniel, Sonny, with a yardstick to silence his barking. Once, while visiting Nana's house for Thanksgiving, my mother shared that when she was a girl she would kneel in front of the picture window every day after school, waiting for her mother to walk down the street and home to her family. My mother's feelings landed on me with a thud—a mixture of sadness and longing that was intense and confusing. Her emotions always flowed into me as if through a psychic uncut umbilical cord.

My mother wasn't a latchkey child—her own grandmother lived with them and spent hours teaching my mom how to keep an immaculate house, a talent she desperately tried to pass on to my sister and me. But despite the contact with her grandmother, the anxious attachment my mother had with her own mother led to feelings of dependency that she struggled with all her life. My mother simply felt safer with a man around the house. By the time women's liberation was in full swing, she had stopped working as a teacher and was a stay-at-home mom with three children under the age of four, a reality that sealed her dependent status for another twenty-five years.

Many years later, in a rare conversation about my father's murder, my mom told me that the two of them had felt an extra level of foreboding about this trip—in fact, they had spoken openly about their discomfort in bed the night before—but that they'd ultimately dismissed it as a silly fear. Perhaps because of this, she had asked my brother, Phil, to stay overnight with us in Brewer rather than return to his dorm. On that evening, when all hell broke loose, I was grateful to have my brother at home.

2

Murder

Amy Banks

New Orleans, 6 p.m.
April 12, 1979

My father checked into the Hyatt Regency, a five-star hotel adjacent to the New Orleans Superdome, around six p.m. The Hyatt had been built just three years earlier as a high-end hotel and conference center designed to attract tourists from around the world. The French Quarter, the heart and soul of New Orleans, was just a few blocks east, while a few blocks to the west sat the Guste Public Housing Project and Erato Street, where Isaac Knapper and Leroy Williams lived. After settling into their room, my father and his colleague, John Hakola, exited the hotel through the Loyola Avenue entrance, turned left, and walked the few blocks to dinner in the French Quarter.

This was my father's first trip to New Orleans, and although he had traveled the world, it was easy to see how the posh hotel and chic Poydras Plaza shopping area disguised the lethal danger lurking just outside the doors. The Hyatt Corporation had created the perfect storm, long before Hurricane Katrina. They had built a luxury hotel and conference center adjacent to a notoriously violent housing project, encouraged tourists to fly in from around the world to take advantage of the city's unique music, food, and Southern hospitality, but failed to alert their visitors to the peril they faced as soon as they set foot outside the complex. The threat was so real and so clear, in fact, that the hotel administration not only had instituted a policy that required hotel workers to use a security escort when walking to the parking lot after dark, they also had hired a perimeter patrol a few weeks earlier to circle the almost three-mile route around the hotel and the Superdome in an effort to keep muggers from preying on visiting tourists. They were fully aware of the extensive criminal activity in the area surrounding the hotel but chose not to warn their guests—not even bothering to make a simple suggestion that they take a cab to dinner or avoid certain streets after dark. My father had no idea the risk he was taking when he and John decided to walk back to the hotel from the French Quarter after dark.

After dinner at Sam Wilson's on Bourbon Street, my father and John meandered through the French Quarter, talking shop and admiring the historic architecture. Though they were on one of the great party streets in America, my father had nothing to drink that night. This didn't come as a big surprise—he almost never drank. In fact, the only time I ever saw him take a drink was eight months earlier, when one of his closest friends collapsed and died from a massive heart attack in the backyard after playing badminton with my parents. I walked into our house and saw my father standing at the top of the stairs, his body and face wracked with grief, throwing back a shot of whiskey in an attempt to settle his nerves. Among his colleagues, his penchant for requesting a glass of milk at cocktail parties was legendary. John had had two drinks with dinner, but by the time the two of them arrived back at the Hyatt Regency, any effects from the alcohol had long since dissipated.

It was an April night in New Orleans, not yet steaming hot, and as they strolled through the French Quarter casually chatting about the buildings, there is little doubt that he and John looked exactly like tourists. They may as well have had bull's-eyes painted on their backs. They turned right off Bourbon Street on to Canal, a main thoroughfare that divides the French Quarter from the Central Business District. After walking four blocks, they turned left on to Elk Place and then continued south on to Loyola Avenue, entering an area around the Hyatt Regency and the massive Superdome that was still under development. It is the street on which my father would die.

April 12, 1979, 9:15 p.m.
New Orleans
500 Loyola Avenue

As my father and John approached the hotel, just a few feet from the safety of the revolving-door entrance, their paths were blocked by two young Black men demanding money. I can easily imagine the wide-eyed shock on my father's face as he heard the words, "Give us your wallet," and realized that he and John were being robbed. I can imagine his confusion and then terror as the surreal became all too real. His response—"You've got to be kidding"—was classic Dad. In his role as assistant to the university president in the late '60s, he was admired for his ability to find common ground between the faculty and the restless, demanding students. He was a very cerebral guy, and even as the adrenaline began to race through his body, preparing him to react to the danger, his mind would have been asking questions. What is going on? What do these guys want? Why are they doing this? The one standing closest to my father was carrying a chrome-plated pistol. These guys were not kidding.

If things hadn't escalated so quickly, my dad almost certainly would have handed over his wallet holding thirty-five dollars and a blank check from the Bangor Savings Bank already signed in thick red marker. Money wasn't a big deal in my family, and it wasn't because we were rich. We lived on my father's salary as a professor at the university and the course or two he taught in the summer to make some extra money. Despite this, I never heard my parents argue or even discuss money. Finances just didn't hold the kind of complicated energy that I felt in some of my friends' families. You had some, you spent it— not outrageously, but generously—when and if it was needed. My father wouldn't have fought to keep the money he carried in his wallet. He was simply taken off guard. John fought the unarmed second assailant, and half-running, half-crawling, fell into the Poydras Plaza entryway. In sheer panic he screamed, "Help, police!" repeatedly. He heard a single gunshot as the first assailant fired his weapon directly into my father's face, the gun so close to his skin it left gunpowder residue around the wound in his left eye. The bullet traveled through his brain and came to rest at the juncture of his head and neck. At his second cervical spine, the bullet severed his spinal column, effectively paralyzing him. He collapsed like a rag doll on the sidewalk at 9:15 p.m., dead.

3

SHOCK

Amy Banks

Brewer, Maine 11 p.m.
April 12, 1979

The sound was unforgettable. The guttural, high-pitched screaming that woke me from a deep sleep was foreign and utterly terrifying. It was the soul-crushing wail heard in horror films and in movie scenes of women who are in the earliest stages of a deep, dark, disbelieving grief. It was both disorienting and clear; something was gravely wrong. I heard voices and footsteps as I walked slowly up the two flights of stairs from my bedroom and was flooded by the memory of my brother mistakenly and tragically stepping on our new kitten on these very same steps just months before. At the time, I had climbed this same route to find the poor little kitty seizing, her body flopping from side to side before falling dead on the landing in the doorway. My parents and brother were watching, helpless in the face of the life-and-death battle the kitten was fighting. The same frantic energy entered the house the night my father was murdered, just a thousand times worse. Halfway up the stairs I ran into Joanne, a dear friend of my parents. With no preparation, her face twisted in pain, she blurted out, "There's been an accident—your father has been shot and killed."

It was a simple, direct statement that would forever change my life. All experiences would now be filtered through this new lens, but in that moment there was no place to hold it in my brain or body. Nothing had prepared me for that devastating statement. And so my mind made a rapid association with a recent *McMillan & Wife* episode that I had watched with my father. In it, a masked gunman had stormed a restaurant, opening fire with an automatic weapon and killing a number of guests, some in mid-chew, others while they scrambled to flee the carnage. In the absence of any concrete details about my father's murder, my brain decided that this was how my father had died. Strangely, after the actual details of his killing became known, the image of the gunman storming the restaurant never disappeared—it still sits in my head, alongside the details of what actually happened. After hearing Joanne's stark words, I didn't scream or cry, and she didn't offer a hug, or even an "I'm so sorry." There would be no comfort for any of us that night, or in the days to follow. Joanne had always been a gentle soul—her husband of sixty years recently described her as an angel. The explanation for her carelessness was simple: shock. By the time we met on the stairs she had known about the murder for at least forty minutes, and she had already entered the freeze state biologically designed to protect her from pain that is simply too overwhelming to bear. Only years later, as a psychiatrist, did I fully understand how traumatized everyone in our lives had been that night. The news of my father's death was like the sudden volcanic explosion in Pompeii, an entire community left frozen in place.

I passed Joanne, and as I climbed the rest of the stairs the screaming grew louder. I could see that it was coming from a body on the couch. My mother was collapsed in agony and was rolled into a fetal ball, delirious with grief. The screams and moans were punctuated with simple angry demands, a resolve to hold on to her life: "This is not true, Ronnie is coming home," or, simply, "I want my mother." Her anguished words echoed throughout the house for the rest of the night as other frozen bodies sat beside her, trying to offer comfort. I walked into the kitchen and found my brother, Phil—suddenly the "man" of the family—leaning against the stove. He and I locked eyes in a desperate stare. No words, just a deep, knowing hug. I, too, wanted my mother.

But my mother was gone, swallowed whole by a lethal cocktail of denial and agony, simultaneously ingesting and regurgitating the unfolding horror. One minute she was a young child screaming for her mother, who had died from breast cancer just two months earlier. The next moment she was a wild animal desperately calling out for my father, repeating over and over, "It can't be true." She was psychotic with shock and grief, oblivious to my brother and me, who were hugging in the kitchen, and to my eight-year-old sister alone in her bed just down the hall, who was no doubt listening in terror to the chaos outside the door. My own body shaking, I approached the couch where my mother's spent body was sprawled with an arm dangling off the edge, her eyes red and swollen and wide with fear. My stay-at-home mom was now a widow at forty-five, left alone to care for four children—two in college and one on the way. For a split second her eyes focused and an unfiltered voice asked, "What are we going to do?" I heard a voice reply, "We'll be okay," and only seconds later realized that the voice was my own. Murder changes the core of who you are and what you expect out of life. Of course there is the usual grief and loss of a beloved family member, the missed graduations and weddings, the missed pep talks and late-night conversations. But when the loss is paired with unspeakable violence, there is no place in your psyche for it to land. In the shock, the fear, and the terror, the body floods with overwhelming levels of epinephrine and norepinephrine. The periods of numbing and the flashbacks to the violence all change the core of a person. Patterns of reacting or collapsing or overcoming, wallowing in misery, or hiding from further pain all become seared deep in one's body.

For the rest of her shortened life, my mother would start most of our conversations by updating me on the latest tragedies around town. The boys who drove ninety miles an hour off a bridge in Bangor, killed instantly, body parts all over the highway. The episode of domestic violence in northern Maine that ended in the beating death of a mother and her five-year-old child. Her mind scanned the world for tragedy, pulling it in as though it were reassuring, comforting: "Bad things do happen to good people—I am not alone." Other times it seemed as if this was the only way she could talk about the crack in her soul, the perpetual open wound in her heart inflicted the night my father was murdered. For me, that evening of April 12th was the day my life turned on a dime. Gone were the carefree days of worrying about two hundred basketball shots a day, or my latest chemistry test. There was no mental free space to hang out with my friends, or to talk about being a seventeen-year-old with the mundane disruptions in friendships, the ups and downs with your boyfriend, the prom at the end of the year. My day-to-day life had taken a back seat to a new survival strategy. I believed my role was to be strong for my mother, to not break down. Her vulnerability was palpable; my vulnerability was hidden behind a wall of responsibility. As my father was being lowered into the ground in a majestic, sea-blue casket, my mother's knees buckled and for a few moments—with my brother and me each grabbing an elbow—she had to be held up. We reminded her that it would just be a few more moments, and with that reassurance, her legs stiffened and she made it through the rest of the burial.

Could we have gotten through it if I had decided that I didn't need to be stoic, that I didn't need to "take care of everything"? My guess is, most likely. But one of the devastating impacts of truly traumatic loss is that it cements relational patterns in place. From that moment on, my future role in all relationships would be clear: I would be needed, and I would be strong. This pattern is so rigidly wedged in place that I could probably get a rock to need me—and not just a pebble, but a strong, self-sufficient boulder.

Through that long night, the house filled. Uncle Gordon and Aunt Kay, my mother's only siblings, raced up coastal Route 1 from my mother's childhood hometown of Camden. Gordon, a lifelong military man, had been back in Maine about a year, having returned from his post in North Dakota to help care for his mother dying from breast cancer. For my mother, who felt safer in the presence of a man, his return was a gift. I reached out to my assistant basketball coach, Linda. Years later, she told me that she could tell the minute she picked up the phone that something was terribly wrong by the faintness of my voice. She rushed to our house from across town and stayed through the night. Minutes and hours ticked by with no hope for sleep but very little to do—we had no distraction from the horror. Someone called Wellesley College, where my older sister, Kate, was sleeping far from the trauma at home. Wellesley officials decided not to wake her in the middle of the night, since no flights would be leaving Boston's Logan Airport until the next morning. They shared the news with her first thing and then drove her to the airport. When Linda and I picked her up, she emerged from the plane with puffy red eyes that were identical to my mother's. Those eyes were becoming a very familiar sight. But I still hadn't shed a tear.

By early Friday morning, my mother had settled enough to think about Nancy, who had spent the night alone in my parents' bedroom. When my mother and I entered, Nancy was sitting up in bed, eyes wide and afraid. The image still breaks my heart—my towheaded sister, dressed in red and white Winnie the Pooh pajamas and sitting stiffly against the wall, covers tossed about, clutching her light blue blanket. Who knows how long she had been awake, what she had heard, what scars she would have from the overwhelming fear that must have over-taken her body during that long night? What is known is that a relational template was cemented for her that night as well: traumatic abandonment. It emerged in boyfriends who weren't good enough for her but whom she couldn't leave, and in an underlying fear of losing people that fuels a commitment and loyalty to her friends that is unshakable.

4

A Final Goodbye

Amy Banks

The days following the murder were gruesome. Spring break started the day after my father was killed, and that year it was filled with death rituals. While the funeral would be closed casket for the public, family members had a private viewing of the body. Kate and I, along with my coach Linda, went together to the Philip Piper Funeral Home with no warning or preparation for what we would find there. Nothing could have prepared me for the sight of my dad, his long body dressed in a new blue suit and white shirt, lying peacefully against the shimmering white silk of the coffin.

A couple of weeks before his trip to New Orleans, I had turned in my junior research paper on, of all things, embalming. So now I had way too much information about what his body had been through between the time he arrived at the funeral home and the state in which I saw it now: neatly laid out for public viewing. His skin looked as though it had been covered with tanning spray. From my research I knew that this orange tint was from the makeup used to cover the translucent white skin left after his blood had been drained and replaced with embalming fluid. My eyes focused on a large blob of the makeup that covered the delicate area on his face between the side of his nose and his left eye, where the bullet had entered. I couldn't take my eyes off it, feeling angry and critical that the mortician hadn't done a better job of patching him up.

The casket was closed below his waist, and as I stood over him with no idea about what to do or how to act, I became obsessed with his feet. My dad had enormous feet—size 15, sometimes 16 depending on the particular shoe. He could never walk into the local shoe store—where the largest size carried was a 12 or 13—and pick up a new pair; instead, he had to order them from a specialty catalog, and this was long before online shopping was routine. His shoes would arrive by mail in long boxes, and when he pulled them out they always looked unnatural—much longer than they were wide, like the long pickerel we caught at camp in the summer. And then my eyes began to fixate on the horrifying sight of his hands. My father was a chronic nail-biter and cuticle-picker, which was a shame given his long, slender fingers. What were now sticking out of the end of his sport coat were cheap plastic replicas with wide fingers that looked as though they'd been dipped in a chalky, pale orange paint, the nail beds puckered with an extra layer of dye. I stared at them for a long time, infuriated. I didn't know how to say goodbye to this version of my father, and I was far too traumatized to do anything more than simply turn around and walk out of the room. No tears shed, no reality sinking in.

To this day, I have haunting nightmares that my father wasn't shot in New Orleans, that it was simply a case of mistaken identity, and that he's somewhere in the world waiting for me to find him. I wake up with a glimmer of hope that is immediately replaced by a lump in my throat as the truth of his murder rushes back in. Some nights I go to sleep hoping for the dream, for the chance to see him alive and anticipate the relief of a reunion. Some days, that connection with him—seeing his smile, his walk—is actually worth waking up and having to replay the traumatic loss all over again.

Four days after her complete collapse, my mother rose from the couch for a Jackie Kennedy moment, determined to "meet your father at the plane one last time." His body arrived in Bangor on Monday afternoon, carried in the cargo hold of a passenger jet along with the luggage. When my mother arrived at the airport, the entire history department at the University of Maine was waiting in grief-stricken silence in honor of their fallen colleague, a moving tribute of respect and admiration.

For weeks after that, my family would gather in the living

room to read the daily mail filled with cards and letters from all over the state and country. Some contained shocked, intimate words from close friends of the family, but there were also letters from students who had taken classes with my father, or from old teachers who wrote to share a sweet story or memory of my father from his days as a student in one of their classes. The governor and many high government employees who knew my father from his work as the Chief Historian for the state on the Indian Lands Claims case sent respectful letters on official State of Maine stationery. My kindergarten, first-, third-, and fourth-grade teachers all sent condolence cards. Reading each person's shock at hearing about this "senseless tragedy" was strangely comforting.

The food and flowers began to pile up even before my father's body arrived back from New Orleans. Casseroles and salads, cookies and cakes, bread and beverages, cut flowers and formal arrangements sent from neighbors and friends trying to "be there" for my family in some measurable way. How odd it was to see piles of food in the kitchen, none of it made by my mother, the best cook I have ever known. During the first few days after his death everyone who entered our house was in a dazed state, just trying their best to get through another day and attend to life's basic tasks. Severe emotional trauma can steal your will to live and eating takes a back seat to breathing. The gifts of food allowed us to eat without thinking.

The day before the funeral, my high school softball team had scheduled a scrimmage, and I needed to play in it. It was easy to convince my mother that Dad would have wanted me to play, that he would have wanted us to go on with life, to be productive. That part was not a lie, but truth be told, I had to get out of the house and get away from the pain that was crushing me. As I slipped into my uniform I realized I couldn't find my softball glove anywhere. The tantrum that followed was dredged from the very core of my being, and it was clearly not about the loss of my softball glove.

When I reached the field, I settled into my usual position

at shortstop and tried to focus on the game. But every time I turned my head, I saw my father standing where he always had, at the fence beside the dugout. And every time I saw his image, I had a split-second reprieve from a conscious awareness of his murder, followed quickly by the realization that he was, in fact, dead and gone. I played softball for two high school seasons after his death and regularly saw him in that same spot, waiting to give me a batting tip or compliment me on a good defensive play. But if I blinked my eyes he was gone, leaving a pit in my stomach.

The day of his funeral was unseasonably warm for April, with bright, blue skies. To this day, the first brilliant spring day leaves me feeling restless and morose. While those around me have an extra jump in their step as they anticipate the arrival of spring, I feel weighted down and terribly sad, actually longing for a few more weeks of winter.

Stretch limos pulled into our solidly middle-class neighborhood an hour before the service. This would be my first limo ride, and it only added to the surreal feeling of the moment. Oddly enough, there was a fair amount of laughter in the car during the drive, part of it at the ridiculousness of the moment, the irony of driving to the funeral in a limo rather than in our Chevy Impala. But much of it was a very familiar Banks coping strategy. My mother's frequent pep talk when things were tough was, "Honestly, if you didn't laugh you would cry." It was certainly true on that day, and I believe that if any of us had started crying, we might never have stopped.

My family wasn't religious in any sense of the word; we weren't even spiritual. My parents believed that each of us would make our own decisions about religion when we were grown up and developed the mental ability to understand the complexity of religion both personally and historically. Nevertheless, the service was held in the Newman Center on the University of Maine campus in Orono. Although built for Catholic members of the community, the Newman Center was the perfect spot for the funeral, for one simple reason: It didn't look or feel like a church. (I dreaded the thought of entering the dark, smothering churches I had visited in the past, with their depressing music and sweet incense.) It was light and airy, with large floor-to-ceiling windows that allowed the sunshine to be as essential to the service as the eulogy. By the time we entered the building, it was already filled to capacity.

In Bangor, Maine, the murder of a local professor was big news, and as our limos pulled up in front of the Newman Center, the front lawn was dotted with news media hoping to film our grief-stricken family as we arrived for the funeral. The same group was camped outside as we exited the building. Later that night we watched ourselves on the evening news, which only made the entire day feel even more bizarre.

When we walked inside, we were ushered into a small room, then marched out just before the service began. It made for good theater: The family of the murdered professor in a state of shock and grief walking down the aisle like guests at a zombie wedding. Just before we were escorted to our front-row seats, a contingent of VIPs emerged from another room. Maine governor Joe Brennan and former governor James Longley were seated in the front, just to our left. It registered in my young mind that this was not a run-of-the-mill funeral, but I wasn't able to grasp that the mourners were a reflection of the man my father had been and the role he had played in his community and state. He was valued in so many different arenas outside our immediate family. To the outside world, Dr. Ronald Banks had died. To me, he was just my dad.

And then, rather abruptly, the rituals were over and life marched on. This was a shock of a different sort. It wasn't that people had stopped caring or had gone into denial about the tragedy, but once the eulogy was given, the body buried, and the food eaten, there was nothing left to do but to get back to everyday life. This was long before victim-advocate groups or compensation funds; in mid-central Maine, no one knew what steps were needed to recover from the violent death of a loved one. My shell-shocked family was left to rebuild our lives with very few outside resources. I returned to school and immediately sensed the awkwardness and tentativeness of my friends and teachers, who simply didn't know what to say or how to help. At home, nothing felt normal. My mother's grief stayed raw and overwhelming for many months after the murder. I was always relieved when I heard the sobbing stop and the back door close early in the morning as my mother headed over to her friend Polly's house two doors down. Polly was the widow of the friend who had died playing badminton in the backyard that fall. They were two young widows with children to care for and hearts to heal. I would wake up with no parent in the house, worried about my sister Nancy, knowing that she needed a functioning mother right then. I longed for those days of utter, frustrating chaos that I had once rebelled against. The house was quiet now, but it wasn't a peaceful quiet—it was a heavy, angry, devastated quiet, with bodies going through the reflexive motions of life, isolated but overflowing with emotion, minds obsessively spinning the details of the murder over and over and over again.

As April turned to May, with the days growing warmer but no more comforting and the structure of daily life barely propping up our shattered lives, the *Bangor Daily News* printed breaking news: An arrest had been made in the murder of Dr. Ronald Banks. The accompanying photo was of two men. On the right was the accused: a young Black man, his face serious and slightly resentful, his torso twisted to one side by the cuffs holding his hands behind his back. On the left side of the photo was John Dillman, the arresting agent and the New Orleans Police Department homicide detective on the case. Dillman was white and well built, and with his curly hair and full moustache, he bore a fair resemblance to the actor Tom Selleck. The killer now had a face and a name: Isaac Knapper.

5

ARRESTED

Isaac Knapper

The day I was arrested for murder began earlier than most. The sun was barely starting to rise on May 19, 1979 at 5:45 a.m. when I was abruptly woken up by sounds of men screaming at the top of their lungs. It felt as if I had been dropped into a terrifying nightmare. When I opened my eyes, I found myself staring directly into the barrel of a gun. In fact, the small room I shared with my brothers was filled with cops, each pointing a gun at my face. They yelled, "Get up now!" but I was confused and my mumbled "What?" was met with more violent screams to "Move it!"

My brother Larry, sitting up in bed, stared at the cops, wide-eyed and motionless. As I stood up, feeling particularly vulnerable in only my underwear, I could see my momma just outside my bedroom door demanding an explanation for this early morning raid. The cops spun me around, forced my hands behind my back, and snapped the handcuffs so tight that they painfully pinched my wrists.

One of the cops told me that I was under arrest for murder. My head spun as he read me my rights. I had no idea who I was accused of murdering and who had identified me as a murderer. As the cops dragged me to the door my momma protested my innocence, emphatic that they had made a mistake. Momma asked if I could get dressed first, but the cops told her that she could bring my clothes to central lockup. I sat in the back seat of the cop car, bare legs sticking to the vinyl seat and my heart racing. I didn't understand what was happening. I hadn't killed anyone, but these words kept running through my mind: *I am going down for murder. I am going down for murder.*

That day in May 1979 changed my life forever. At central lockup the cops decided to book me—still in my underwear—and I began to worry that this horrible mistake was not going to be fixed quickly. I was caught up in a whirlwind of conspiracy, but at sixteen years of age, I had no idea what had been set in motion.

Central lockup was terrifying. I was locked in a filthy, cramped holding cell with ten men. At the rear of the cell there was a single toilet, stopped up with feces, its seat covered with urine and vomit. I was glad I did not have to go to the bathroom because I could never sit on that toilet seat. I was kept in the holding cell for twelve long hours. We were given cold bologna sandwiches that I couldn't bring myself to eat in that nasty environment. I sat on the floor, men crowded to every side, and the smell of urine so intense that it made me cringe.

An older guy sitting on a bench asked my age. When I told him I was sixteen, he replied, "Dang, Red, you must have killed someone famous to be in here with us." I told him that while the cops had charged me with murder, I was innocent. He asked who I was supposed to have killed, and I told him I had no idea. He rifled through his pocket, flipped me a dime, and recommended I call someone who knew what was going on.

I called Momma from an open pay phone on the wall. She was worried that someone would hurt me and acted as if it had been ten years since I had been taken away, rather than a few hours. I assured her that I was fine, and that everything would be all right—though I had no belief that either was true. She told me that she was waiting to hear from a lawyer, that she would be down to get me freed as soon as she could. Just as I heard the guard calling my name, she said exactly what I needed to hear: "Stay strong. I know you did not kill anyone."

The guards took me for fingerprints and mug shots. They made me hold a black card with white numbers to my chest and forced me to turn left, then right, then to the front, each time snapping photos. I remember thinking that even models don't have this many pictures taken at one time.

The next six months of my life were a living hell. I soon learned that first degree murder was a "no bail" offense, which meant that I could not go home before the trial, even if I had the money to post bail. Within twenty-four hours of my transfer to a holding cell to await trial, my momma came to visit. It felt like the best day of my life.

She asked if I was all right and if they were feeding me well. Her third question was predictable—was I reading the Bible. I said I was and she grabbed both of my hands tightly, looked me squarely in the eyes, and started praying. The fifteen minutes allotted for our visit felt like fifteen seconds. After hugging her goodbye, I assured her that I would be okay. As I watched the guards escort her out, my heart sank. I thought of the promise I had just made—that I would be all right. It was a lie as big as the one I had just told her about reading the Bible.

Immediately following my momma's visit, the guards marched me straight to the interrogation room. The questioning resembled any you might see on TV shows like *Law and Order* and *CSI*, with one difference. For security reasons (or so I was told), I sat at the table in the same clothes I had been arrested in—my underwear. The man who entered the room to interrogate me would change my life forever.

Detective John Dillman, a well-built man with dark hair and a moustache, entered the room, introduced himself, and launched into a lengthy explanation about why I had been selected to stand trial for first degree murder. He occasionally glanced at the thick manila folder he was holding as he reported that he had eyewitness reports that I was the triggerman who had killed Dr. Banks. When I tried to calmly tell him that I hadn't killed anyone, that I had never met Dr. Banks, and had no clue who he was, tension escalated in the room. And then things got ugly.

I was only sixteen years old, sitting in my underwear with my hands cuffed behind my back, when Detective Dillman called in another cop, Scarface (appropriately and frighteningly named for the long scar running down his right cheek). One of them put a bag over my head and then both of them beat me repeatedly and severely. After the beating, they dragged me down what felt like five flights of stairs, the handcuffs biting deeper and deeper into my wrists and my head bouncing off the steps. Though I was far too weak to put up a fight, I willed myself to remain conscious. I remember thinking about my first boxing coach, Percy Pugh, asking me as a young boy if I could take a punch.

Finally, we reached the first floor and they stopped dragging me. I could barely make out the solitary confinement cell in front of me but heard the creak of the rusty door opening and felt my body being hurled into the dark cell headfirst. They slammed the door behind me and I listened to the echo of their shoes on concrete as they walked away.

After struggling in the pitch dark to find the rusted metal bed, I crawled onto it and lay there listening to the sound of my labored breathing. My ribs were so sore that even shallow breathing was excruciating. I realized that it was time for pain and me to become good friends. In fact, I believed I would die from my injuries in that wretched space.

I could taste blood in my mouth and my arms felt as if they had been pulled out of their sockets. Eventually, despite the pain I closed my eyes and drifted off to sleep or lost consciousness, I am not sure which. I eventually awoke in the dark cell, where I remained for another two weeks, naïvely believing that since I had not confessed to the murder, Detective Dillman would realize he had arrested the wrong person.

After sitting for a while in the dark, rat-infested cell, my fear diminished, replaced by a burning anger—and I embraced that rage as a drowning man embraces a life raft. The handcuffs were still attached to my wrists and I kept thinking that someone needed to come back and take them off so I could fight back. This time, I'd actually throw some punches.

Two weeks later, without warning, I was transferred to the old parish prison where they housed me with the adult inmates in B-4. I heard some of the inmates identify me as "Nap the Boxer." They either knew me from the projects, where I had built a reputation as a Golden Gloves boxer, or they heard my name from the six o'clock news where the Banks murder and my arrest were making headlines on a regular basis.

In the parish prison I began to feel increasingly ill from the interrogation beatings. During this time of physical anguish, I cried out to God as I had never done before, asking Him to send my momma to get me out. Within a couple of hours, my prayers were answered as my momma arrived; however, she was rudely told I wasn't allowed visitors. My momma has a will of steel and the prison administration grossly underestimated her. She went all the way up the chain of command to the captain and demanded that she be allowed to visit her son, emphasizing that I was a sixteen-year-old boy locked up with grown, violent men.

The captain relented and allowed my momma to visit. The moment she laid eyes on me and saw what bad shape I was in, she cried and reported my dire condition to the captain. I was rushed, along with a guard escort, to Charity Hospital, where the doctors found fractured ribs and blood clots compressing my lungs, which made it hard for me to breathe. They inserted tubes on both sides of my chest to drain the blood, and I spent another eight weeks in the hospital recovering from the inter-rogation beatings.

When I returned to the parish prison, Detective Dillman was waiting for me, ready to question me again about the murder. When I denied any knowledge of the killing he did not beat me again, but he returned a few days later to offer me a deal. I had heard from other inmates that an acquaintance who lived in my neighborhood, Leroy Williams, had also been charged with the murder. About a month or so before the arrests, Leroy and I had gotten into a physical fight after he had laughed at one of my friends. Somehow, Detective Dillman heard about this altercation and decided to use the "the enemy of my enemy is my friend" theory to pit us against each other.

Detective Dillman announced that he knew Williams had been the shooter and that I could walk free that day if I only signed the statement he held in his hand confirming that Williams was the shooter. Admittedly, this offer sounded good to my teenage ears, but two things worried me. First, Dillman wouldn't let me read the statement before I signed it; and second, I had no idea whether Williams was the triggerman because I hadn't been there. It wasn't long before I heard through the prison grapevine that Williams, after being threatened with the death penalty or life in prison, confessed to the murder and identified me as his accomplice.

So there I sat, in an adult prison, being offered my freedom in exchange for a lie. I remember thinking at that moment that if Detective Dillman had spent as much time, energy, and effort in pursuit of the real killer as he had spent pressuring two teenagers to confess to a murder they did not commit, none of this would have happened. But of course that was not the case, and I had two options before me: sign the statement or risk going to prison for life. I didn't sign the statement.

6

GROWING UP

Isaac Knapper

Guste Public Housing Project
New Orleans
1971

I was nine years old and just another Black kid living in a New Orleans housing project on the south side of town. The Guste Public Housing Project was a place of despair where few people, if any, survive to become somebody. At the time, I was busy being a kid, and all I knew was the life around me; the world outside the projects wasn't much of a concern for folks living in them. My life revolved around 2429 Erato Street, a three-bedroom house that somehow managed to shelter my momma, two brothers, and seven sisters—ten kids growing up with little room, less food, and no father. My momma worked three jobs for as long as I could remember. Even though we lived in the projects, my mother was never on welfare. She worked very hard, and after the bills were paid she always spent money on her children so we could have a few nice things.

My sisters and my brother Larry had a different father than Corneal and me. We, the two youngest kids, were Knappers and our father was never around when I was growing up. Ernest Lee was the father of the older kids, a big man of 260 pounds and six foot five. He suffered a tragic death at the hands of New Orleans's finest, or worst, as I recall them. He was at a bar one night, and someone slipped him a tainted drink. On his way home he was stopped by a New Orleans police officer who thought they had some drunk old nigger. Ernest was a tough guy and he did not go down without a fight. Six policemen beat him and even then he did not quit. He threw their guns and nightsticks out of range to make it an even fight. Eventually he was subdued and two days later he died from a fractured skull and brain hemorrhage. A brief investigation into the cause of his death, and the motives for the beating, reported that Ernest Lee had been drunk, had been resisting arrest, and had been behaving in a disorderly way. Apparently, according to Louisiana law, these accusations justified beating a man to death.

I was just six or seven at the time, but this act of police violence that took Ernest Lee from his family was seared into my mind. At the cemetery my sister Maggie was so devastated that she threw herself onto his casket.

Poverty in the projects was a way of life—it was the very air we breathed—but like kids everywhere, we had our own dreams of what we wanted to do when we grew up. We just never knew that obtaining our dreams would be so hard. When I was nine, I knew what I wanted to be: the boxing champion of the world.

Scotty Foreman was my first inspiration. He had already won twenty-five amateur fights and two Louisiana Golden Glove lightweight championships by the age of seventeen. He was only a teenager, but to me he was everything I wanted to be—a boxer. We trained together at the Black Cobra Boxing Gym, named for the Cobra himself—Percy "Black Cobra" Pugh.

Scotty—my sister Hazel's boyfriend as well as my idol—had also grown up in the Melpomene Projects, but you would never have known it. He was smart, devilishly handsome, and well-dressed, and he had class. Most importantly, he was an exceptional boxer—he could jab, slip, and punch with unbeatable power. Even in the projects no one dared to fool with him. Scotty was the icon for amateur boxing in New Orleans, and he was where I wanted to be.

I had the amateur boxing title on my mind every day, and I believed it was my ticket out of despair in the projects. Truth is, I didn't think there was much else I could do. I used to think that being a fighter just came naturally. When I first visited Cobra Gym, it was filled with boxers, young and old, doing workouts that I had no idea needed to be done before you could actually call yourself a boxer.

The first thing I noticed was the noise: the high-speed thumps of fighters jabbing the speed bags and the deep thuds as they pounded the heavy bag. The boxing ring was well worn, but as far as I was concerned, it was simply marvelous. A rectangular red pad in one corner of the ring had EVERLAST printed on it in bold white letters. In the opposite corner was a similar navy-blue pad. As I stood in the gym for the first time, I felt a wave of emotion wash over me. I couldn't wait to get in there and box.

Like a lot of teenagers, I was pretty sure I knew it all, but I found out before too long that I had a lot to learn. Over time, with Scotty's guidance, I learned that boxing required relentless desire and an equally relentless training schedule. We jogged nine miles every three days. In my mind, I was already the champ, the "K.O. Kid," the best fighter in New Orleans.

The day I met the Black Cobra, Percy Pugh, I didn't recognize him, which was just as well—if I had known I was in the presence of boxing royalty, I would have been overcome by nerves. Scotty introduced me as his girlfriend's brother, Jerry (a family nickname). Percy asked me if I thought I could fight, and I immediately replied, "Yeah, I can fight!" He then asked me if I could take a punch and I replied enthusiastically that I could.

"I hope so, because if you can't, you'd be better off in another line of work," Percy said, laughing at his own remark. "You look tough for a kid. Let's see what he's got. Scotty, dress him out."

I dressed in an old T-shirt, a new pair of gray shorts, and my old sneakers—the only pair I owned. Scotty showed me how to wrap my hands so that I didn't break them when I was punching the other guy. Then he held up his palms and told me to hit them. We repeated this a number of times, and then we moved on to shadowboxing, and Scotty taught me how to jab, slip, and move.

I began to realize that I knew very little about what it took to become a boxer. Scotty told me to watch him and to do what he did. He flicked a left jab so fast that I never saw his fist. He bobbed and weaved, shifting backward and forward. And then it was my turn. I began to move, sticking, jabbing, bobbing, and weaving just as I had seen Scotty do a million times. Suddenly, Percy positioned himself right behind me, watching every move I made.

"Hell, Scotty!" Percy exclaimed. "This kid can box!"

I stopped for a moment to hear what he was saying, but he told me to keep going. I overheard them commenting that I had quick reflexes. Percy moved over in front of the mirror and said, "Now watch, kid." He set his feet, then threw a flurry of punches that were so fast and fluid that I was able to feel a slight breeze. "Keep sticking your jab out. Keep moving."

The Black Cobra was magic to watch in action: the almost imperceptible movements of his darting fists and his head bobbing up and down and up and down. His hands seemed to move at the speed of light. He had such grace. Hell, he *was* grace! Percy and Scotty showered me with praise for the rest of the day. Percy called me a natural, but when Scotty explained what that meant it went right over my head. With only a few weeks of live training under my belt I entered my first boxing tournament as a member of Percy's team.

Typically, we would fight according to our weight class, with the smaller fighters boxing first, followed by the bigger guys. Being on the smaller side, I expected to fight first or second, but for some reason I had been scheduled last. Percy suggested that they often saved the best for last, but I knew he was just trying to build up my confidence. I smiled and said what he wanted to hear: "I'm gonna knock this boy out."

Percy laughed and gave me a high-five.

After Scotty won his bout, he was all smiles, raising his arms and waving to everyone in the building. "It's your turn, Jerry. Go in and get him," he told me. My match came up a few minutes later, and to say I was cool would be a straight-up lie. I knew I was tough and fast, but after I had sparred a few times, I realized that boxing wasn't just about beating up a kid. How I thought about fighting kids my age and weight quickly changed.

My first sparring session had been with Scotty's younger brother, Glen. Glen was close to my age, and he could fight. My strategy had been to ambush him as if he were a total stranger, but it wasn't that easy. Although Glen was the first person I had ever punched, the punch was with great big gloves that weighed about fourteen ounces and were used to protect young kids when boxing. Landing a good punch with those fluffy pillows was not easy.

Percy always coached me to my limits, seeing to it that I worked with kids who could stay away from my punching power. He would pair me with guys like Elston "Sugar" Davis, who was two or three years older than I was, fast and elusive. I couldn't hit him. My everyday sparring partner ended up being my cousin Timmy, who was about seven months younger than I was and had a boxing style similar to Elston's. Sparring outside my comfort zone allowed me to develop the skills I needed to become a complete boxer—the person who I imagined in my dreams was beating everyone.

As I anxiously waited for that first fight to start, I kept looking at myself in the mirror to be sure I still had on my brand-new, sparkling-pink boxing trunks and the new, bright-white shoes that Percy had purchased for the whole team. Wearing these cool trunks, rather than my old high-tops and gray shorts, was a source of pride. I was fascinated by the white stripes that streaked down the sides.

I felt almost giddy with excitement and anticipation. I was the man! But what if I failed? What if my opponent was like Elston, fast and good enough to beat me? At this point in my training, I hadn't learned anything about "positive thinking."

It was finally time to put all my worries aside. As I walked past the audience, I saw my number-one fan, Momma, along with my sisters and my little brother, Corneal, who didn't have a clue as to what was about to take place. Momma was radiant with pride. All seven of my sisters were yelling at me. "Don't let him hurt you, baby! If he hurts you, just lay down so they'll stop it!" Standing in the ring before my first fight I heard my momma scream, "Don't get hurt, baby, please!"

As I made my way to the ring, Percy stayed right behind me, which boosted my confidence. Only two Cobra boxers had lost that day, and I didn't want to be the third. I was so excited and nervous at the same time that I had goose bumps, but I still felt warm, and when I stepped through the ropes and into the ring, I felt vicious. Where was this coming from? I could be mean, but this was something else. I craned my neck over the ropes to see my family, hoping they could see how cool I looked. I threw my hands up in the air, just as I had seen Scotty do many times, acting as if I had already won. Percy pulled me back into the corner and sat me down on a wooden stool.

"Okay, kid," he said, full of emotion. "Remember what you learned. Keep your hands up. When the bell rings go out with that jab flickin'. Get off first. Keep that jab in his face. The first punch is always the best, so get off first. Keep your mouth shut and breathe through your nose."

Ding! Ding! Ding! And there he was, my first boxing opponent, Ricky Valentine. When he was introduced as the fighter from the blue corner, weighing in at eighty-six pounds and fighting out of the Desire Boxing Club, he just sat there. When I was introduced in the red corner, at eighty-five pounds, fighting my first fight for the Cobra Boxing Gym, I leapt to my feet and bounced around in an exaggerated effort to look cool. Roars from my corner sounded like a pack of hungry lions that made the feast in front of me look even more scrumptious.

When we met in the center of the ring, I thought Ricky looked worried, and I tried to look mean to intimidate him. But, heck, we were both kids. When the bell sounded to start the fight, I ferociously attacked him. Left jab snapping, just as Percy had always instructed. My first jab didn't connect, but then one finally hit home, and Ricky backpedaled, taking cover. Then I dropped a missile on him that landed dead on target.

Ricky lost his balance and went down—my first knockdown in my first real fight. The referee sent me to my corner, and when I turned around, I expected to see him still on the floor. But he was up long before the end of the ten count. Still, at the end of the match, with Ricky and me standing anxiously in the middle of the ring, waiting for the decision, the referee finally held up my hand. It was my first victory as a boxer, and it was special.

I didn't want it to end. I didn't want to take off the pink trunks and white shoes, and I didn't want the intense adrenaline rush to stop. But my night was done. I left the ring and joined Scotty, Percy, my momma, my sisters, and Corneal. I was on cloud nine, convinced that nothing could stop me.

In 1971 I didn't know anything about respect, or the fact that it had to be earned. But it's a word that I now use to define my relationship with these two most influential men in my life. I grew up fast in boxing, but there were times when I wish I had known then what I know now. I couldn't anticipate that boxing would help prepare me for the hard punches that life would send my way. But, heck, Percy had described me as the best he had ever seen at my age. What more could be said?

Scotty and I jogged regularly together during those early years—nine miles to Tulane Stadium and back home. During our runs I asked questions and he patiently answered them. At times we ran in silence and watched the city change its complexion. Scotty, who was only seventeen at the time, became my hero and role model, the father figure I desperately needed.

7

FRIENDS IN NEED

Isaac Knapper

For Christmas in 1974 my momma surprised me with a mini-bike. She gave it to me a week early but wouldn't let me ride it till Christmas morning. Just as I was revving up my bike, I heard a couple of minibikes ripping through the projects. My two best friends, Ricky Gordan and Randy Bell, were racing through the projects on their own minibikes. Ricky and Randy always seemed to have a pocketful of money—more money than they should have had. It wasn't hard for kids in the projects to find a way to make some easy money, but I didn't know the "hows" required and my two friends never told me where they got it. It seemed, at the time, that we were always together; however, now it seems clear that while I was laying concrete with my uncle, they were "making money." Soon after getting my bike, I figured out that I could charge a quarter for all the rides people requested rather than giving them for free. I saved all of the quarters I gathered for gas, a cold drink, or a burger from the new Burger King on Tulane Ave.

One day I heard Ricky's scooter headed my way. He ditched the bike in a hurry and rushed to my front door. As he ran into the house, he told me the cops were looking for him and Randy. Randy was in the hospital with another asthma attack, I told him, and I asked why the cops were looking for them. His answer cleared up the mystery of where they were getting their money.

"Man, you are making money working with your uncle and all, so me and Randy needed some money too. I stole my brother's gun from under his mattress, and me and Randy went to that new Burger King on Tulane. I gave the gun to Randy, because he kept telling me I was too short, and I held the door while he went in and robbed them. I know they didn't see me, because I was holding the door. They only saw Randy."

In those days, Randy and I looked very similar—both with red hair and freckles. In fact, both our mothers used to call us twins when we were younger. This became a problem when the cops came to my door looking for Ricky and Randy. I suggested that Ricky stay at my house to avoid the police and the very next morning we heard a car stop in front of the house. I naïvely told Ricky that since I hadn't done anything, I would answer the door and find out what was going on. I slowly made my way to the front door, allowing Ricky time to flee through the window.

The police officer asked my name and if there were any adults or "babysitters" around. I gave him plenty of attitude, knowing that I had done nothing wrong. When I told him I was there by myself, he said simply, "Isaac Knapper, we are placing you under arrest."

When I protested, saying I hadn't done anything, he shot back: "What about the Burger King you robbed?" and then, "Where's your buddy, Ricky? The one that helped you rob the place." I denied knowing anyone by that name and stated emphatically that I had not robbed a Burger King, which was met with, "You're lying, boy."

As they drove me down to juvenile detention, I realized that they had mistaken me for Randy because we look so much alike. I was held in detention for four hours before my mother was able to come and pick me up. I now had a Juvenile Court date in the near future.

When I finally returned home, Ricky sneaked back into my house and the two of us went over to Randy's, who had just returned from the hospital. When I described what the cops had done to me, I could see the fear in Randy's eyes. So I decided to take the blame for the robbery. Randy protested, but it was clear to me, even as a young kid, that Randy could not survive juvenile detention; he was too sick. I did, however, demand that

Randy never rob anyone again. He replied, "Don't worry, Nap, I ain't never robbing any place again."

Ricky turned himself in the next day and ended up getting two years' probation. When my court day came, I pleaded guilty to the robbery. At fourteen I had convinced myself this was the right course of action, to protect my friend, but when the police started asking me questions, I couldn't answer them. Riding home from the police station, my mother made it clear she knew I was lying for someone. Someone should have told me that I needed to let my friend pay for his crime, but I had no guidance of this kind, and I took the fall. I talked myself into it by minimizing the impact of the detention center and thinking that in just a couple of months, the three of us would be back together again, riding our scooters and hanging out in the boxing gym.

When my hearing came up, one Burger King employee positively identified me, while a second said she didn't think I looked like the perpetrator at all. However, I sealed my own fate when the judge asked if I was pleading guilty and I said yes. The judge showed no mercy for my stupidity and sentenced me to fourteen months in LTI, or the Louisiana Training Institute.

It was just before Christmas when I found myself sitting in the back of a sheriff's van with my hands and feet cuffed. There were a few other guys in there with me as we drove to LTI— better known as "Scotland" in Baton Rouge. This is where boys were kept for "crimes against the public." My big heart had gotten me into a big mess. I certainly wasn't thinking of what I would face in detention when I decided to help Randy. And I suspected that Randy and Ricky were not sitting around feeling bad for me. They were free to enjoy life. I was beginning to regret my decision.

My angry thoughts were interrupted periodically by the van going way too fast around corners, throwing all of us around inside. The two-hour drive to Baton Rouge reminded me of the trips my family would take to Mississippi to visit my grandma. Momma would drive us, and I would escape into the scenery of the countryside. When we finally pulled up in front of Scotland, with its tall fences lined with razor wire, I was hit by the smell of horses. Guards on horseback wandered through the grounds. I was pleasantly surprised that it did not look or feel like a prison. There were no doors or bars and you could wear normal everyday clothes. We were put into dormitories with thirty or forty other guys, and I realized this would take some getting used to. Home was cramped with eleven people, but this wasn't home—there was so much yelling and chaos all around me.

I was surprised to find that I knew many of the guys already, and I also quickly realized that I would need to establish my reputation. Every time a new inmate arrived, there was so much talk. Guys wanted to be bad and talk the talk, but they usually couldn't walk the walk. Guys mouthed off and the next thing you knew there was a brawl. Older guys pushed their weight around, simply because they were bigger, but almost no one talked bad to me. The word got out quickly that I "didn't take no shit from anyone."

I was pissed off and missing my family, and Scotland was just the pill I needed to escalate my anger. In New Orleans the different sections of town are called wards, and in Scotland the dorms were a mixture of kids from different wards. My dorm held boys from the Third and Ninth Wards; the Ninth Ward, however, had a couple of bigger guys who were bullies, while the Third Ward still needed a leader. Guys looked up to me right away because I was a boxer from the Melpomene Projects.

The Magnolia Dormitory, where I was housed during my time in Scotland, was run by guys from the Ninth Ward who dictated where other residents could sit. I didn't know and I didn't care where they wanted me to sit. Hector, one of the leaders from the Ninth Ward approached me one day and asked me to identify myself. Full of attitude, he claimed I was sitting in the wrong place. In Scotland, fights were settled in the bathroom. In fact, the bathroom would become my ring for the next fourteen months. Hector didn't fight me directly, but he sent in another, bigger guy who lasted about forty-five seconds. After I had torn his ass out of the frame, the rest of the guys backed up and wanted to talk. Even Hector wanted to be my friend. I was the new badass from the Third Ward, and we were back on top.

After I beat a guy who had stolen my friend's shampoo, I was sent to the hole for two weeks. The administration was sick of me kicking people's asses, so they placed me in ankle cuffs for forty-five days. The cuffs were a permanent fixture on my legs; even when I was sleeping, they slept with me. The only time this arrangement changed was when I took a shower—one cuff was removed to make sure I did not slip and fall.

Dealing with ankle cuffs was extremely humbling for me. However, the powerlessness I felt only fueled a deeper anger. I already had the Knapper-Lee temper, one that everyone in my family knew about. The cuffs were like pouring gas on a fire. One day a new, big white guy was in "my" shower without asking me. Given that I was recently out of the cuffs, I decided to use my head and try to talk with him. He informed me that he would use "his" shower any time he wanted to. I just backed down, warning him that he should know who he was fucking with. He continued to provoke me later in the TV room, saying that if I wanted trouble, he would bring plenty my way. That was the straw that broke the camel's back.

That night, when he was sleeping and snoring, I plugged in a hot iron, spit-tested it to see if it was ready, and then proceeded to iron his face. He woke up screaming, begging me to stop, but I kept after him, trying to place the iron on other parts of his body. As a result of this incident, I was sent to the adjustment center, another name for the hole, for two months.

Sometimes things don't work out how you expect them to. In fact, Big Boy got a medical discharge because of the burns I caused, and I was certainly not going to get early release for good behavior. That, however, was the price I paid in order to develop a reputation that would protect me. I did not spend all of my time at Scotland fighting, and when things settled down,

I was able to do more constructive things. I've always been a good athlete, and I played running back on Scotland's football team, forward on the soccer team, and even a lifeguard at the pool. Looking back, I realized that the house parents would give me more important jobs in order to use my reputation to their advantage.

The time in Scotland wasn't all bad. One night a guy named Spacehead came to a couple of us, all excited. He held out his hand and showed us a key. We had no idea what it opened and so we systematically went from door to door, trying to find the lock it belonged to. Much to our surprise, it opened the only door between us and the free side of the dorm. That night, once the house parents put us to bed, a small group headed to the girls' center. New girls were held in Scotland for three to six weeks until they were sent to a more permanent holding spot in Pineville. It took us three nights and three tries to actually get to the girls' dorm, climb the tree, and cut the bolts on the window screen. When we finally opened the screen, one of my buddies was pulled into their room as if he had been sucked in by a vacuum. The girls acted as if they had not seen guys in years. Once inside, we had only twenty minutes before we had to be back in our dorm for count. As we retreated, we saw a light go on in the girls' dorm and realized the house mother was in the room. After being present for midnight count in our own dorms, my friends and I started getting fresh, even putting on cologne for the trip back to visit the girls. As we approached the girls' dorm a second time, I saw that the lights were still on and could see some of the girls signaling us to turn around. Then we saw the house mother come to the window and—darn!—she saw us.

We sprinted back to our dorm and just as we made it back, our lights came on and Mr. Anderson began counting again. Shortly after this episode all the locks were changed and it was back to business as usual. Boring. There were a few fun times when my momma, sister, and Ricky would visit me. During those times we were allowed picnics outside, and Ricky always made a point of letting me know how grateful he was for what I had done for him in taking the rap for the crime.

As my fourteen months came to a close, I was a year older and Scotland had done nothing to calm me down—in fact, it had made me more sure of myself. I knew I would never return and, in fact, I never did return. I wasn't a bad kid, but I had developed into a tough kid. I couldn't wait to get back to boxing and the rest of my life. It was January 1978, and I had no way of knowing that I would be free for only seventeen more months.

8

HOME

Isaac Knapper

When I was finally released from Scotland, Momma picked me up in a new car. Not just any car but a GTO. When she fired up the engine, I thrilled at the rumble of the old muscle car. It had bucket seats and a gear shifter in the console. It started out slow, but then Momma drove it fast, as if she were an Italian race-car driver. The ride home was cool and helped me forget Scotland.

When I arrived home, I was so happy to see the projects, having spent the last two Christmases and New Years in detention. Hazel made my favorite food—chicken and dumplings and banana pudding. Everything felt so beautiful—my favorite food, my family, and my home—all the things I had ached for while in Scotland. I felt like a little king, but I had not yet learned my lesson.

I was enrolled at Carter C. Woodson Jr. High, and there were a lot of things I wanted to do—most notably, boxing. I knew I had gotten bigger and stronger while I was away, and I longed to start training again with Scotty and Percy. But being free after fourteen months of incarceration also meant that I wanted to do other things too. In Scotland I had learned from the best thieves how to make some quick change. I didn't want to return to detention; however, I had difficulty focusing on my school studies. The only gym I could make time for was the school's gym, every morning during first period. P.E. was so boring that eventually I simply stopped going and watched the girls' gym class.

Unknown to me at the time, one of the girls I was watching was also watching me. In the middle of gym class one day, I got hit by Cupid's arrow at the exact same time I took my eye off a ball. They both hit me at the same time—me staring at her eyes as the ball hit me upside my head. A small girl with very large breasts grabbed my attention. I tried to look cool after the ball hit my head. She smiled, introduced herself by her nickname, Sequin (her actual name was Dece), and told me I was cute. I replied, a little defensively, "You like me, but you don't know me." She said she did like me, particularly my freckles. We agreed to meet after school to walk home together.

Sequin's family was not from the projects. She lived on the other side of Jackson and La Salle. We held hands and talked in front of her house for about a half hour before it became clear to me that it didn't bother her that I was a kid from the projects. We walked home together for the next month, and I was even introduced to her parents and brother. Her brother wouldn't talk to me, believing that I was a troublemaker from the projects. Truth is, he was right. When we walked home, Sequin's brother would run to their mother and say that Sequin was with the freckle-faced red boy from the projects. When her mother learned that I had been detained in LTI she would not let Dece see me. So, in order to see each other, we had to sneak around.

I was, by now, a tough guy who could back up my talk if I had to, and I would do it whenever I had to. By this time my attitude had gotten too bad to keep a job. So Ricky and I began "till tapping." Ricky would enter a store, acting like a nitwit and stuttering his speech, when the cashier had the cash register drawer open. When she leaned forward to better understand what Ricky was saying, I would grab the cash and race to the door, where Larry would be waiting and watching for security. We were hitting one or two cash registers a weekend. One weekend, Ricky decided we should go till tapping at Sears, which, in retrospect, posed two problems. The first was that it was on the fifth floor of the building—too high up to make an easy getaway. The second issue was the cops. By the time I had made it to the first floor, there were plainclothes cops everywhere.

They grabbed me and off I went to the police station again. They called Momma to come get me, and this time I ended up with six months' probation.

I wasn't paying attention to much of anything and was headed back for more trouble when my sister Hazel intervened. She arranged for Scotty Foreman to have a talk with me. He wanted to know why I had given up the gym. He told me that I could go places with boxing, but instead I was just paving my road back to jail. He reminded me of the Junior Olympics, which would be held in six months, and said I had the skills and talent to win it all. That put my mind back where it needed to be. I now had a goal—to work toward that championship. This talk with Scotty signified a major change in me. I started back to my road work, and I put aside the till tapping.

In my first fight back, my opponent was a white guy with bright red hair. He took two eight-counts in the second round, and then his team robbed me of a knockout by throwing in the towel. I was officially back, but this time was different. I was able to throw combos more effectively, just as Percy had taught me. As far as organized boxing was concerned, I was nearly invincible. Little did I know that this would be the last fight I would have in the free world for almost fifteen years. The black cloud that had been following me was now directly over my head.

At the time I loved dogs (and still do). Ricky, Larry, and I started catching stray dogs and keeping them in an old abandoned house on the other side of the projects. Feeding them was difficult, and we looked for food everywhere. I loved them so much, in fact, that at times I would save some of my own food to give to them. One day, as we were leaving the doghouse on our minibikes, we ran into a group of girls we wanted to impress. Ricky decided to show off and, in so doing, crashed his bike on the street and was hurled to the ground. Across the street I heard another boy laughing at him and it didn't sit right with me.

Leroy Williams was a tough guy that lived across the street

from me in the projects. I didn't like him laughing at Ricky, who was nineteen but looked fifteen. So I went over to Leroy and hit him with a straight right, knocking him to the ground. This ass-whipping wasn't anything unusual that day, but a few months down the road it would cost me my life as I knew it. Leroy Williams was thrown into the middle as my whole world started slipping away, and I never saw it coming.

It was now 1979, and I had just four months left to breathe the air of the city. If I'd had any idea of the train that was about to hit me, I would have done something to stop it. At the time, I thought my life would go on forever, back on track, as I was, for the Olympics. Instead, my stubbornness was about to plunge me into another world—one which had no escape.

9

AWAITING JUSTICE

Amy Banks

In the first few months after my father's death, I feared my mother would never emerge from her shock and grief. But she did, slowly and with a newfound sense of pride. Having never paid attention to the family finances, she was forced to take over the money management and did so in her typical compulsive style. As each bill arrived, she promptly placed it in a manila folder neatly labeled in her flowery, cursive penmanship and paid it long before the due date. Insurance policies, report cards, and other important papers were organized in folders and filed alphabetically in a large black metal cabinet in the basement. It was as if the external order would calm the internal chaos and disorientation she was dropped into when the only man she had ever loved had been taken from her.

Occasionally she commented on how much better she was at keeping our financial lives together and that she should have been doing it all along. Of course that was true, but it was said with a confusing edge of anger and bitterness. A classic example of my father's lax attitude around money was found in his wallet when he died—a blank check already signed in bold red marker. Under his watch we were one stolen wallet away from the poorhouse. Once my mother discovered my father had been killed "on the job" while at an academic conference and she would receive monthly workmen's compensation checks in addition to social security benefits, her panic over financial ruin passed. Her competence fueled a new confidence. She proudly balanced her checkbook to the penny every month and even planned a budget.

Right after my father's death, Phil moved back home, and

within a few weeks Kate returned to Wellesley College just west of Boston. As summer progressed my mom began having some good days. The early morning sobbing stopped and she started cooking again. My mother was funny and charismatic, and her many friends rallied to her side for long walks, cups of coffee, and an occasional cry. Her two siblings lived an hour away in Camden, and she often loaded Nancy into the car and drove down Route 1 to Lincolnville to spend the day with her sister, Kay, on the gray, sandy beach of their childhood. My mom nursed a thermos of hot coffee while sitting on a beach towel in her one-piece suit while Kay chain-smoked cigarettes and worked on her bikini tan. Nancy played safely on the beach, chasing seagulls and building sand castles.

For long stretches we heard little from the New Orleans district attorney office. Isaac Knapper and Leroy Williams had been arrested in May. Because the crime was a capital offense, they were not eligible for bail and were awaiting trial in prison. Most of what we heard was filtered through our local lawyer, Joe Ferris. He protectively buffered us from the legalese about motions and hearings that did not impact us in any significant way. However, as the summer days grew shorter and the air crisper, the criminal trial loomed large. We had no way of predicting the uptick in fear, anxiety, and grief that would come with the process of justice. In the weeks before the trial, the house again swelled with pain and tension as the details of my father's murder were discussed whenever any two or more adults were present. The news coming from the DA's office was spotty and confusing: though two suspects had been caught, the case was not strong. I remember overhearing whispers about a key eyewitness the detectives could no longer find. The DA's office warned us that the two young men might be acquitted, not because they were innocent, but because the prosecution was unable to build a case against them "beyond a reasonable doubt"—the standard of proof needed in a capital murder trial. We needed to brace ourselves for the horrifying reality that justice might not be served and that these boys could be released to kill again. And then, suddenly, about a week before the trial, the mood lifted as the DA shared the great news that one of the arrested men had agreed to turn state's witness in exchange for a lesser sentence. Suddenly, our team was confident that the outcome of the trial would be in our favor and that the man they were certain pulled the trigger would be convicted. In fact, because he was being tried as an adult for first degree murder he could be sentenced to death.

After my father's death, Phil became the man of the family at twenty and was chosen by my mother to travel to New Orleans with my mother's brother, Uncle Gordan, for the trial. I was just three years younger than Phil but had grown up fast in the months since my father's death and begged my mother to let me go. I needed to be there to see the photos of my dead father on the sidewalk, to watch his killer enter the courtroom, and to smell the humid New Orleans air. I needed to sweat in the place that my father had died. I was furious when she said I could not go.

After all these years, I am convinced Phil should not have gone to the trial. He once shared with me how difficult it was to stay seated with his father's killer an arm's length away, how hard it was to control his anger, how badly he wanted to hurt Isaac Knapper, kill him even. Over the years, this anger has eaten him from the inside out as his life energy has been drained in a futile struggle to manage the post-traumatic stress symptoms he developed from the murder and trial.

10

Isaac Knapper

As I sat in a cold, cramped, concrete holding cell at four a.m. on the day of my trial, my mind played the nightmare over and over again. My life was spinning out of control and I was in a state of shock, grief, and confusion. My best friend, Ricky Gordan, had been going to testify for the defense today—for me, and he was killed for it. Ricky had called my momma the day he was shot by Leroy Williams's brother, Jackie. He shared with her that he had heard in the neighborhood who had actually killed Dr. Banks. He assured her that it was not me and promised to visit the following day and share everything with her.

After the phone call, my momma went across the street to Leroy Williams's mother's house and repeated the conversation she had just had with Ricky. Clearly, what Ricky had reported threatened Leroy and Jackie. Later that night Ricky and his brother Donald were standing outside their house when Jackie Williams approached them on the sidewalk. As Ricky was saying, "What's up?" Jackie shot and killed him, then pointed the gun at Donald and pulled the trigger. Without saying a single word, Jackie turned and ran away.

Donald was lucky—when Jackie pulled the trigger a second time, the gun only clicked, as he had run out of bullets. But Ricky lay dying on the sidewalk, a bullet in his heart. Donald was on his knees, holding Ricky, weeping and yelling for help, but by the time EMTs arrived, Ricky was dead. In disbelief, Donald watched the ambulance drive off with his brother's body less than an hour after they had been simply standing and talking together.

What could possibly have prompted this killing? There was

no feud, no bad feelings between the boys. In addition to the phone call to Momma, there was some speculation that Ricky had gone to the police, telling them he knew who had shot Dr. Banks. Donald picked up the torch for his fallen brother, contacting my lawyer and saying he would testify in my defense. To this day I still wonder why Ricky was killed. Why Jackie would have risked life in prison to hide what was already known in the neighborhood. I had so many unanswered questions. Had someone ordered this killing? Who was really behind it? Who said I did this? What was going to happen to me today?

Already exhausted from days without sleep, I dropped to the floor, my mind floating back to the image of Ricky doing his tricks. I smiled, thinking of how his head used to bob up and down when he boxed.

I had been in Orleans Parish Prison for five long months— every day I faced strangers in a place I didn't belong, in a city without a friendly face. One day while I was waiting for the trial, an attorney came to see me. His name was Mr. Zibilich and he announced that he would be defending me in the murder trial. I was a little worried because I thought I smelled alcohol on his breath. At the time, I knew very little about lawyers and believed he would know what he was doing, and because I was innocent, he would succeed in getting me acquitted. Long after the trial was done, I was enraged when I learned that Zibilich had extracted extra money from Momma to keep me out of jail.

Mr. Zibilich had an associate, Clyde Merritt, who visited far more often and seemed genuinely concerned about me. He shared with me that the prosecution really wanted to convict someone in this case because Dr. Banks was such an upstanding citizen. They also wanted to showcase the great work of the police department. Mr. Merritt understood that I was innocent and, despite being "second chair" in my trial, he fought tooth and nail with the judge. In fact, during my trial, the judge threw him out of the courtroom because he objected too much. He was the wrench they didn't want jamming the gears of the kangaroo court.

I had waited for this day since all the madness began. Finally, I would be tried for a murder I knew nothing about and certainly could not have committed. I didn't even own a gun! One of the worst things about the upcoming trial was that I still didn't know all the details of what had happened. Sure, I was hearing some things, but what I found out at the trial rocked my world.

Sitting in that holding cell, I did not know that others had been arrested for the murder but that I would be the only one tried or that the key witness was someone who hadn't come near me in the neighborhood. I also didn't know that if they found me guilty, they could kill me—or worse, send me to prison for the rest of my life. Surely the jury would not find an innocent kid guilty without proof. Mentally I rehearsed what I would say, but nothing felt right. If I saw it, it didn't look right; if I touched it, it didn't feel right. I couldn't eat because it didn't taste right.

It was 8:30 a.m. when I entered the courtroom wearing the jail clothes I had worn all week. I was not allowed to wear a suit or nice clothing—my jail clothes, no doubt, were intended to remind the jury that I was not only bad but guilty. I sat beside my attorney, who said very little to me during the course of the very short trial. The jury was already seated—ten Black people and two white people. Back then I didn't even understand the significance of that ratio. Suddenly the clerk came in and announced for all to rise and said, "Here comes the judge." Once everyone was seated the show began.

The trial was not fair by any standards. In fact, it more closely resembled a Broadway production starring the prosecutors, David Paddison and Rick Fornet, and their primary witness, Leroy Williams. Paddison and Fornet had fabricated a case against me; the whole trial was a sham, and it was my life they were fooling with. I suspect that everyone from the DA's office already knew my ass was cooked.

Judge Frank Shea ruled over my trial, and if I had to think of one word that best described him as a person and a judge it would be *abomination*. Judge Shea, who chain-smoked from the bench throughout the trial, had earned a reputation for being unfair and unjust long before I entered his courtroom. He took pride in belittling female lawyers from either side of a case to the point where many refused to come back to his courtroom. David Paddison, who had become a lawyer just seven months before my trial, led the prosecution team.

The first prosecution witness was Dr. John Hakola, who had stood face to face with the shooters six months before. Dr. Hakola was a professor of history at a major Northeastern university. His mind was filled with centuries of historical facts; surely he would remember the details of that traumatic night just six months earlier. Less than three feet had separated him from the killer. He had even shoved one of the robbers. He was as close to the assault as Dr. Banks had been. I fervently believed he would bring the truth to the stand, and that he wouldn't have the rehearsed answers the DA's office was counting on to convict me.

11

The Trial

Amy Banks and Isaac Knapper

Amy –

John Hakola had been walking beside my father, and he was closest to the Hyatt Regency entry when the robbers approached. He should have been the prosecution's best witness, but during the scuffle, his glasses fell off and he was extremely nearsighted. Without his glasses, the world became a vague haze. He could identify sizes, shapes, and colors but lacked the clarity to identify the specifics of a face. On the stand he was visibly shaking and his testimony was tentative.

Returning to New Orleans to testify was his worst nightmare and it killed him—literally. John was not only a colleague and a friend to my father but also a mentor who had nurtured his intellectual growth from graduate student to assistant professor at the University of Maine. When John returned to the university after the murder, he was wracked with survivor guilt.

At the time of his death my father was teaching his usual classes in U.S. and Maine history, leaving his students without a professor just as they were preparing for finals. John stepped in and took over the classes as well as my father's other university responsibilities—essentially, holding two jobs at a time when he desperately needed to rest and recover from the trauma he had survived. The increased workload, on top of an already genetically loaded cardiac system, was a ticking time bomb.

John never talked about the terrifying attack in New Orleans with anyone, not even his wife. The emotions were trapped within him, no doubt eating away at his body and soul with each obsessive thought and wave of grief. He felt deeply that it was his duty to return to New Orleans to testify, but the fact that he did not have a clear image of the killer's face haunted him. A year after the trial he suffered a massive stroke in the area of his brain that controlled speech, locking the trauma within him for the rest of his shortened life.

It tortured him to be so close to the assailants and yet have such little recollection of their faces. His testimony was halting and unsure. (The following exchanges are taken directly from the original trial transcript documenting the full court proceedings.)

Hakola: The one with the gun, I think, was about my height.

Paddison: How tall would that be, sir?

Hakola: About five-nine. And he had what was, I guess probably, a sailor hat down to his eyes. It appeared to be a grayish thing; it wasn't clean white, it was just a grayish thing. And he had a bandana starts [sic] below his eyes, dark color....

Paddison: What was his approximate weight, Doctor?

Hakola: A hundred sixty-five. Right around that area. I am a hundred and seventy-five; I'm not sure he's quite as heavy as I am. Dark pants, as far as I know.

Paddison: Do you remember what color shirt he was wearing?

Hakola: I think it was black.

A few moments into the testimony, Paddison instructed Dr. Hakola to leave the witness stand and approach the table where Knapper was sitting. He stood directly in front of the young man who had allegedly killed his friend. After Dr. Hakola returned to the witness stand, Paddison continued his questioning:

Paddison: Doctor, would you say what you just said on the record, please?
Hakola: Yes. He's the same height, as I remembered, but I cannot positively identify him.

Paddison: Doctor, is it the same approximate build?

Hakola: Yes.

Paddison: Doctor, when all this transpired, were you scared?

Hakola: Panicked.

Paddison: How old was Doctor Banks?

Hakola: Maybe forty, I think.

Paddison: Doctor, is there any doubt in your mind, whatsoever, that the heavy-set man was the one with the gun?

Hakola: As far as I know, yes, he was the one with the gun.

Paddison: And doctor, one last question. Is the same physic [*sic*] as the defendant's, like that of the man who had the gun?

Hakola: Pardon?

Paddison: Is the defendant's physic [*sic*], who you just identified, like that of the man that had the gun?

Hakola: Yes, yes, it is.

A few minutes later, in rebuttal, Paddison continued:

Paddison: Doctor, do you recall the complexion of the man that had the gun in his hand?

Hakola: Middling.

Paddison: Pardon?

Hakola: Middling and Black, he was Black.

Paddison: But as compared to the other individual. When you say middling, what do you mean?

Hakola: Well, not really very, very dark or very, very light.

Paddison: Could the complexion have been that of the defendant?

Hakola: Yes, it could.

Hakola's testimony did not identify the actual killer, but it did narrow the field down to two men—one slim with darker skin and a sailor hat; the second, with lighter skin, carrying a chrome-plated pistol. The prosecution was not worried that John Hakola had only a vague recollection of the murderer because their second witness, Leroy Williams, had made a deal. After five months of denying he was at the scene of the crime and just one week before the trial began, Williams signed a plea agreement—he would avoid a first-degree murder charge by pleading guilty to manslaughter and testifying that Knapper had been the shooter.

Leroy Williams was called to the stand as the second witness. He was tall and thin with a dark complexion. After taking the oath and identifying himself as a seventeen-year-old high school freshman at Booker Washington School, he shared his story of the night of April 12, 1979. This was the heart of the prosecution case.

> Paddison: Leroy, I'm going to direct your attention to the night of April 12, 1979, and ask you to tell the ladies and gentlemen of the jury what transpired that evening. What happened?
>
> Williams: Well, I was standing in the project.
>
> Paddison: What project is that?
>
> Williams: Melpomene
>
> Paddison: Okay. Go on.
>
> Williams: I was standing in the project, and I met Isaac, and he asked me did I want to go make me some money.

At Paddison's request Williams pointed to Isaac at the defense table and then continued in a faint voice.

> Williams: And he asked me, "Let's go make some money," and I went with him. Well, we went walking down Loyola, I think that's the street, and we saw these two men, and we say, "Let get them two." We went on ahead, and I got on side of one of them, and he went in front of them, and he pulled out the pistol and told the man to give up the money, and the man said, "You got to be kidding." And he shot him.

As the testimony continued, Leroy identified the chrome-plated pistol as the one Isaac had carried and confirmed Hakola's description of the clothing worn by the robbers. In cross examination, Isaac's attorney attempted to raise reasonable doubt about Williams's testimony, highlighting the fact that it was attached to a plea deal with the DA's office that allowed him to plead guilty to manslaughter in order to avoid the death penalty or life in prison.

Leroy's mother, Cecile Williams, followed her son to the witness stand and essentially confirmed Leroy's story. In a brief appearance, she testified that Leroy had told her he had been with Isaac the night of the murder, watching a wrestling match at the Superdome just around the corner from the crime scene at the Hyatt Regency Hotel. She testified that on the night before his arrest, Leroy had specifically said that Isaac "shot that man." There was no mention from either the defense or the prosecution of the conversation between Isaac's mother and Cecile Williams about Ricky Gordon's knowledge of the real killer.

Alan Tidwell, a firearms examiner from the New Orleans Police Department, testified that the bullet that killed Dr. Banks came from the gun found a week later at another crime scene. The coroner testified on the cause of death: "gunshot wound to the head, shot at point blank range." There was little cross-examination of these witnesses, and immediately after hearing the gruesome details of our father's murder, my brother, Phil, was scheduled to identify our father. Mercifully, all agreed this was unnecessary and he was released to watch the remaining trial from his seat behind the prosecution table.

Isaac –

During the investigation of the crime, the only person to identify me as one of the shooters was a young man named Tony Williams (unrelated to Leroy and Jackie Williams). I knew Tony; he had grown up in the same housing project as me, and he and I had been in juvenile detention together a few years before the trial. He was the sole reason I had been arrested. According to the Dillman report—a police record discovered long after my conviction—Tony Williams had been walking on Loyola Avenue the night of the murder. He claimed, as reported in the Dillman papers, that I ran right past him with the gun in my hand. However, when the lead investigator, Detective Dillman, took the stand during the trial, he stated he had tried and failed multiple times to find Tony.

Dillman, by his own admission, could do anything he wanted, go anywhere he pleased, and find anybody he needed. Yet he claimed, under oath that day in court, that he couldn't find his key witness. I suspect that the reason he could not find Tony, who was living in the Melpomene Housing Project at the time of the trial, was that he did not want to. Everyone who knew Tony knew that he was emotionally disturbed and had been from birth. While Tony would accept anything Dillman suggested, he would not be a strong or believable witness on the stand.

Also under oath, Dillman claimed he could not remember the names or descriptions of the three suspects he had interviewed a week after the murder, suspects who had been caught with the murder weapon in the midst of another armed robbery. This happened in a court of law right under the public's nose, and it went totally unnoticed and unchallenged.

Amy –

John Dillman, an eight-year homicide police veteran, took the stand for the prosecution. After establishing his role as the lead investigator at the crime scene, responsible for ordering the photos and gathering evidence, his testimony moved on to the discovery of the weapon and his order to send it to the crime lab. The questioning then turned to the only person to identify Isaac Knapper and Leroy Williams as the assailants: Tony Williams.

> Paddison: Officer, you stated previously that there was a witness, Tony Williams?
>
> Dillman: Yes, sir, that's correct.
>
> Paddison: Do you know where Mr. Williams is today?

Dillman: No, sir, I don't.

Paddison: Since the time of the commission of the offense and the time you spoke to Mr. Williams, have you made attempts and efforts to locate this man?

Dillman: Yes, sir, I have, practically on a daily basis.

Paddison: With any success?

Dillman: No, sir, to no avail.

Paddison: No further questions.

On cross-examination, Zibilich questioned Dillman about two young Black men who had been arrested with the handgun used in the murder a week later—young men that Dillman had interviewed in person.

Zibilich: From whom did you obtain that weapon, S-11, officer?

Dillman: I obtained the weapon from my crime lab. The weapon had been recovered during the apprehension of two subjects, on an armed robbery, by members of the First District.

Zibilich: Who were those subjects? Take a look at the thing (referring to the handgun), it might be able to help you.

Dillman: I don't recall, right off hand, sir, their names.

Zibilich: Would this refresh your memory? [referring to a tag on the weapon]

Dillman: Yes, sir, it will. A subject by the name of Ricky Williams and also a Derek Robertson.

Zibilich: I have nothing further.

Paddison: I have just a couple.

A very brief rebuttal by Paddison established that Dillman had interviewed everyone in the immediate vicinity of the crime over the course of the month-long investigation. At this point, Zibilich re-crossed:

Zibilich: Officer, these Ricky Williams, Derek Robertson—do you happen to know anything about their height, size, or anything like that?

Dillman: I interviewed both arrested subjects, but I don't recall, right off hand, their physical description, no, sir.

Zibilich: Were they Black—?

Dillman: They were both young Black males, yes, sir.

Zibilich: All right.

On that note, the defense rested its case just in time for a lunch break. At 1:30 p.m., Isaac's defense team of Zibilich and Merritt began by calling Joseph Smith to the witness stand. Mr. Smith was a refrigeration engineer who was familiar with the Knapper family from the time he had spent working on their TV set. He testified that on the night of the murder he had been standing across the street when he heard the single shot and saw two men fleeing the crime scene—one "kind of short," and the other "a little taller." The shorter one, he recalled, carried something in his hand that he could not identify because of the distance. In cross-examination the prosecution attorney, Paddison, asked Smith directly, "What makes you think it was not Isaac Knapper?"

Smith: Well, because like I said, two fellows were running, they were dark, and I know Isaac. He's much brighter than those fellows I saw.

In testimony that contradicted both Hakola and Leroy Williams's story from earlier that morning, Joseph Smith did not remember seeing a mask on either of the men as they fled the scene. Debra Dudley then took the stand, saying she had been near the Hyatt the night of the murder walking her sick son to Charity Hospital. She testified to hearing a single gunshot and then seeing three men running toward her. The last one, short and carrying a gun, ran over her baby, knocking him down. She was so scared she turned and ran toward the Hyatt Regency rather than the Charity Hospital.

Ms. Dudley testified that she did not know Isaac personally but had seen him on occasion when he came to a house next door to get a beverage from the cold-drink machine. She testified that Isaac Knapper was not one of the men fleeing the scene; however, she did positively identify Leroy Williams as the tall man fleeing the scene. In the ensuing cross-examination by Mr. Foret, a member of the prosecution, he highlighted the inconsistencies in Ms. Dudley's description of the size, complexion, and number of men running from the scene. He also questioned the timing of her discussion with Isaac's lawyers. Apparently, Ms. Dudley came forward only after a conversation with Isaac's sister, who told her that Isaac had been arrested for the murder that happened on April 12. Despite the prosecution's skepticism regarding her testimony, Ms. Dudley remained firm that, after seeing the picture of Isaac in the paper, she could not identify him as one of the men running from the scene.

The defense next called Cheryl Cockerham to the witness stand. She was an A.D.F. security police, employed by the Hyatt Regency, who happened to be leaving the building around 9:10 p.m. on the night of April 12, 1979. She also testified to seeing three men running away from the crime scene; the one lagging behind was shorter in stature and carried a gun. In cross-examination Cheryl stated firmly that she saw the last man clearly—and that it was not Isaac Knapper. However, she conceded that she did not get a clear view of the other two, but she felt sure they could be identified as neither Isaac Knapper nor Leroy Williams.

Donald Gordan, the brother of Isaac's best friend, Ricky, took the stand next. At the time of the trial he was serving a two-year sentence in Orleans Parish Prison where Isaac Knapper, Leroy, and Jackie Williams were all being housed. His testimony focused on a damning conversation he had overheard between Leroy and another inmate.

Merritt: Tell the jury what you heard.

Gordan: Well, I heard Leroy talking about his charge, you

know, and he say that his mama make him lie on Isaac, in order for him to get his freedom, you know, about this here charge, you know, but he wasn't talking to me, directly to me. He was talking to a dude on the same tier with him about it, so I just overheard.

The prosecution's cross-examination attempted to undermine the integrity of Gordan's report. It focused on the fact that he was a known criminal currently serving time in the parish prison for his second offense for carrying a concealed weapon and that he was a friend of Knapper's and had contact with him from "time to time."

The remainder of the defense came from Knapper's family, starting with his sister Betty Jean Johnson, who had been home in bed the morning Isaac was picked up. The Knapper family was a close-knit one, and they gathered regularly at their mother's house. Her testimony was clear that Isaac had been home with his family all evening and therefore could not have murdered Dr. Banks. In fact, Betty Jean vividly recalled that evening because it was the night her own fifteen-year-old son had been picked up for theft on April 11 and sent to the Youth Student Center on Milton Street, about four and a half miles from Betty Jean's mother's home. On April 12, the day of the murder, she was visiting her son until the end of visiting hours at seven p.m. After leaving the Youth Student Center, she drove directly to her mother's house on Erato Street, a fifteen- to twenty-minute drive, depending on traffic. As was typical for the Knapper family, a large group had gathered to hang out, chat, and play music.

Betty Jean had read about the murder of the professor the day after it had happened; however, the report made no particular imprint in her mind. People were killed regularly on the streets of New Orleans, after all.

Foret: How did you correlate [sic] in your mind that Isaac, that particular night, was at that particular place? What made it stick out in your mind?

Johnson: Because I went and seen my son that day, and the next day was Good Friday.

Foret: But Isaac was there every other night too, wasn't he?

Johnson: Most of the nights he was there.

Foret: So you had to think back a whole month, correct?

Johnson: I had to think the day people was talking.

Foret: How long did it take you, before it dawned in your mind that he couldn't have done it, because he was with you? Did you realize instantaneously, or was it the next day, after you sat there and thought about it?

Johnson: When I realized that it was for that day, for that murder, I realized he couldn't have done it.

Foret: All right. When did you realize that?

Johnson: I don't know, about a day or two later.

Foret: So you had to go back and sit down and think about it?

Johnson: When it happen.

Foret: When what happened?

Johnson: The murder.

Foret: Okay, what I'm talking about is when you found out that Isaac was charged with the murder, okay?

Johnson: Yeah.

Foret: That was the morning after the murder, right?

Johnson: Yeah.

Foret: Okay. When was it that you realized, that you were with Isaac, and he couldn't have committed the murder, how long did it take you to realize that.

Johnson: About a day or two.

Foret: And you had to sit down and think about it?

Johnson: I had to realize it was the same murder, because

I didn't know, I had to realize that's the murder they had him for.

Foret: They didn't give you a date, your mother didn't say— was your mother there that night, that Thursday night?

Johnson: Yes, she was there that Thursday night.

Foret: Who told you about Isaac being arrested?

Johnson: Well, my mother told me. We were together every day.

Foret: And when she told you that he was arrested, did she say to you, 'Hey, wait a minute, he couldn't have been there that night to commit that murder, because he was with us'?

Johnson: Well, I didn't know it till that night, till the next night, after they picked him up, because I went to work.

Foret: Did she say that to you?

Johnson: She just told me that it couldn't have been him.

Foret: It couldn't have been him because he wouldn't do a thing like that?

Johnson: He was at home that night it happened.

Foret: But you didn't realize that for a day or two later?

Johnson: That's because I had forgotten the date that it happened, that it was the same thing, 'cause every day you reading about something.

Foret: Every day you read about what things?

Johnson: Different things that happened.

Perhaps recognizing that he was getting nowhere with the argument that Betty Jean did not know whether Isaac was home on the night of the murder, Foret switched strategies.

Foret: Did Isaac ever hang around the Superdome?

Johnson: Not that I know of.

Foret: You ever know him to walk by there?

Johnson: I don't know.

Foret: Did he have transportation, did he have a car, or usually traveled on foot, or what?

Johnson: He traveled on foot.

Foret: How far is where he used to live with his mother from the Hyatt Regency Hotel or the Superdome?

Johnson: About five or six blocks.

Foret: Excuse me?

Johnson: About five or six blocks.

Foret: So the night that you're saying he couldn't have done it, because he was with you, he was actually five or six blocks away?

Johnson: No, the night that ya'll [sic] have him accused of doing this here, he was at home, playing records and talking, laughing and talking 'cause they were planning on going out of town.

Foret: How far was that from the Superdome?

Johnson: I told you, about five or six blocks.

Foret: So the night that you say you were with him, you're saying he couldn't have been that way, because he was five blocks away?

Johnson: He was in the house.

Foret: You seen him?

Johnson: Yeah.

After Betty Jean testified that she knew of Leroy Williams but did not understand him to be a friend of Isaac's, Foret pressed further.

Foret: Now, when you found out that he was charged with murder, one or two days later, and you realized in your own mind that he couldn't have done it now, at that point, you ran right to the police, right?

Johnson: No, I didn't.

Foret: You didn't?

Johnson: No.

Foret: Who did you go to?

Johnson: My mother.

Foret: You and your mother went right to the police?

Johnson: No.

Foret: Where did ya'll go?

Johnson: My mother got a lawyer.

Foret: Mr. Merritt?

Johnson: Yes.

Mr. Merritt then brought another of Isaac's sisters, Hazel Lee, to the stand. Her testimony was simple and direct. She was with Isaac that night because she, Isaac, and her son were scheduled to go to the country for the Easter weekend that evening. The man who was to take them had some car problems and so they did not end up leaving till the next morning. However, she was very clear that Isaac was in the house with them all evening long. In cross-examination, Foret ripped at the fabric of the family.

Foret: I'm not talking about when the professor was murdered. I'm talking about when your brother was arrested. When your brother was arrested, did you find out that same day that he was arrested?

Lee: Yes.

Foret: After you found out he was arrested, how long was it before you realized that he couldn't have done it? Because he was with you?

Lee: The day the police officers came for him, the morning. I was there. They came to the door for him, and I asked them what day was this professor murdered. He said, "On the twelfth," and I said, "He couldn't have murdered the professor, because he was at home."

Foret: You told the police that?

Lee: No, I didn't tell him that.

Foret: But you realized it when they were picking him up, and this is the same *[close]*-knit family and you didn't tell the police that?

Lee: Well, the police wasn't going to listen to me.

And then Isaac took the stand, a mere six weeks after his seventeenth birthday, with his life literally on the line. While being questioned by his defense attorney, Isaac shared a story similar to the one his sisters had told—that he had been home with his family, listening to music and waiting to leave for a weekend in the country. Isaac denied any role in the robbery or shooting, denied being aware of the weapon, denied a close relationship with or even being with Leroy Williams the night of the murder, denied knowing Ricky Williams, and though he admitted to knowing Donald Gordan, he denied discussing the conversation Donald had overheard between Leroy Williams and another inmate at the parish prison.

In cross examination, Foret was both condescending and aggressive.

Foret: Now, what's the charge that you're charged with, Isaac?

Knapper: Murder.

Foret: Murder. Any particular degree?

Knapper: First degree.

Foret: Do you know what the penalty for that is?

Knapper: No, I don't.

Foret: You don't know what the penalty for first degree murder is?

Knapper: No, I don't.

Foret: If I told you that if you were found guilty of first degree murder, by this twelve-member panel, and their vote would have to be unanimous, twelve jurors, and they recommended a verdict of guilty as charged, guilty of first degree murder, then we would retire for a second hearing and in that hearing, they will choose between one and two sentences; one being life in prison for Isaac Knapper the other being the electric chair for Isaac Knapper, would that refresh you—?

Knapper: I don't know what you mean.

Foret: You don't know what I mean?

Knapper: No.

Foret: You don't understand that you could be electrocuted if you were found guilty?

Knapper: Yeah, I understand.

Foret: You understand now?

Knapper: Yeah.

Foret: When did you come to that understanding, just now?

Knapper: You just told me and I understand.

Foret: You didn't know about that before?

Knapper: No.

Foret: What did you think were the possibilities before I told you?

Knapper: Life imprisonment.

Foret: Life in prison, that the maximum you could get?

Knapper: I believe so.

Foret: So, in other words, when you took the witness stand, just a few moments ago, you weren't even worried about being electrocuted, were you?

Mr. Zibilich interjected again: Your Honor, I fail to see the relevancy, except to show that he's an uneducated individual.

Court: Now wait a minute, don't make a speech, objection is sustained. (*To Foret:*) I believe you have covered your point.

Foret: Yes, sir.

Foret continued: You know, or you knew, Leroy Williams about six months ago?

Knapper: Yeah.

Foret: Now, do you know how old he is?

Knapper: Seventeen.

Foret: Same age as you, right?

Knapper: Yeah.

Foret: Do you know how tall he is?

Knapper: About the same height.

Foret: About the same height as you? How tall are you?

Knapper: I'm six-two.

Foret: You sure about that? Stand up. Okay, you can have a seat. How much do you weigh?

Knapper: About one-forty-five.

Foret: Six-two, one-forty-five. I heard Mr. Merritt say, earlier in the day, that you had done some boxing. That right?

Knapper: Yeah.

Foret: For whom?

Knapper: New Orleans Police Department.

Foret then meandered in his questioning to ask about weight class in boxing, then reverted to Leroy Williams, in an attempt to establish Leroy's tendency to take charge or to be a follower when interacting with others. Appropriately, Isaac's lawyer objected. Finally, Foret got down to the actual day of the murder.

Foret: Now, in this particular night, when the professor was killed; let's start early in the day, and it's Holy Thursday, and I want you to tell the twelve people—the twelve ladies and gentlemen of the jury—from the time you woke up, that Thursday morning.

Mr. Merritt interjected: If he remembers and is reprimanded by the court.

Foret: Start right from when you woke up that morning and tell us what you did.

Knapper: I can't remember.

Foret: You can't remember? Well, let's start from where you can remember.

Knapper: I know that evening I went to the gym.

Foret: What time was that?

Knapper: About 3:30, evening time.

Foret: You and who else?

Knapper: Glen, a dude name Glen, Scotty Foreman.

Foret: How many guys went with you?

Knapper: Two.

Foret: Had you been to work that day, or school, or what?

Knapper: No.

Foret: Were you working or going to school?

Knapper: Yeah, I was going to school.

Foret: Where is that?

Knapper: Warren Easton.

Foret: Did you have school that day?

Knapper: No, we didn't have school that day.

Foret: Did you have school the day before?

Knapper: I believe so.

Foret: Now at 3:30 you went to the gym. Then what did you do?

Knapper: Training.

Foret: You ran?

Knapper: Training.

Foret: How long did you stay there?

Knapper: About an hour.

Foret: What gym is that?

Knapper: N.O.P.D.

Foret: Where is that?

Knapper: On Magazine.

Foret: Magazine, up by the Second District Police Station?

Knapper: Yes.

Foret: How did you get from your house up to there?

Knapper: This guy in a car.

Foret: Now when you left there, what time was it, about 4:30?

Knapper: I would say about 4:30.

Foret: Where did you go?

Knapper: My house.

Foret: Your mother's house?

Knapper: Yeah.

Foret: When you got there, who was there?

Knapper: My sister and them.

Foret: Excuse me?

Knapper: My sister, my brother, my auntie, my momma.

Foret: Why don't you give us the names, that would help clarify it.

Knapper: Hazel Lee, Betty Johnson, Linda Lee, Maxine Lee, Corneal Knapper, Larry Lee, my momma [Clara Lee].

Foret: About seven or eight people?

Knapper: Eleven or twelve people.

Foret: Eleven or twelve people?

Knapper: Yeah.

Foret: Now, when you got there, what did you do?

Knapper: Took me a bath.

Foret: Okay. And after that?

Knapper: Got up on the bed for a little while.

Foret: You went to bed for a little while.?

Knapper: Yeah.

Foret: And what time did you get out of bed?

Knapper: I stayed in bed about thirty minutes.

Foret: What time did you get out of bed?

Knapper: I don't remember.

Foret: Can't remember?

Knapper: No.

Foret: Have you been thinking of that night for a long time?

Knapper: Yeah, since I been up here.

Foret: Since you been in here. I believe you said six months, actually, I think it's more like five months, or whatever. You been in jail at least five months, right?

Knapper: Yeah.

Foret: And every day, every day that you're in jail, you're saying to yourself, "I couldn't have done that because I was home that day." And every day you retrace yourself, and you remember, what you did that particular day, isn't that right?

Knapper: Say it again.

Foret: How many times have you thought about this particular day, Holy Thursday?

Knapper: Holy Thursday we was going to the country, me and my sister, her little boy, and my uncle.

Foret: We'll get to that in just a second. How many times have you thought, have you tried to retrace your activities on that particular night? How many times have you thought about it?

Knapper: While I was here?

Foret: Excuse me?

Knapper: While I was locked up?

Foret: Yes.

Knapper: I think about it almost every night.

Foret: You think about it almost every night. What time did you get out of bed?

Knapper: I can't remember.

Foret: All right. After you got out of bed, what did you do?

Knapper: Me and my brother and my sister and them went up to the back room playing music.

Foret: Playing music.

Knapper: Yeah.

Foret: That's more or less what you do every night?

Knapper: Besides going to the gym.

Foret: But it's not unusual for you to be back there playing music, that night was just like any other night, isn't that right?

Knapper: No.

Foret: Why is it different?

Knapper: We were supposed to go to the country that night.

Foret: You were supposed to go to the country that night?

Knapper: Yeah.

Foret: Thursday or supposed to go Friday?

Knapper: Supposed to go Thursday, but the car broke down so we left Friday.

Foret: Whose car was it?

Knapper: My uncle's.

Foret: You been sitting here the whole day, haven't you?

Knapper: Yeah.

Foret: Been listening pretty close to everything?

Knapper: Yeah.

Foret: Did you hear what that witness say that ya'll [sic] had been planning for two weeks to leave Friday?

Knapper: Yeah, I heard.

Foret: But you say now that ya'll [sic] planned to leave on Thursday?

Knapper: We was. We left Friday. The car broke down on Thursday.

Foret: In your mind, you were planning to leave Thursday?

Knapper: Yeah, as I say, we left Friday.

Foret: Whereabouts in the country did ya'll [sic] go to Friday?

Knapper: McComb, Mississippi.

Foret: How long did you stay there?

Knapper: About three, two days, two or three days.

Foret: That would mean that you came back—what, Easter Sunday? The following Monday, or when was it?

Knapper: Easter night.

Foret: Easter night?

Knapper: Late that night.

Foret: How long were you at your mama's house before the police came and got you, how many days?

Knapper: What do you mean?

Foret: How long, after you got back from the country— Easter Sunday. Let's use that as a starting point—from Easter Sunday, until when were you arrested?

Knapper: I can't remember.

Foret: When you were arrested, how long was it, how long did it take you to sit down and think about it that you were really at your mother's house?

Knapper: I know I was at my momma's house, 'cause that was a special day. We were planning on going to my grand-mother's house.

Foret: In other words, as soon as the police arrested you, you knew?

Knapper: As soon as the police arrested me?

Foret: As soon as the police arrested you, and told you the day of the murder, you knew right away that you couldn't have done it, in your mind?

Knapper: Not right then and there.

Foret: You had to think about it awhile?

Knapper: Yeah.

The testimony switched gears as Foret then began to focus on the gun and the location of the Superdome relative to Isaac's mother's home.

Foret: You never seen this gun before, that Mr. Zibilich showed you a minute ago?

Knapper: Never seen it before.

Foret: You ever carried a gun?

Knapper: No, I don't own a gun.

Foret: How far is your mother's house? You do live with your mother, or you did live with your mother, right?

Knapper: Yeah.

Foret: How far is that from the Superdome and the Hyatt Regency?

Knapper: Seven or eight blocks.

Foret: So, in other words, you're telling these people in the jury, that you couldn't have committed this murder because you were seven or eight blocks away?

Knapper: I couldn't have committed this murder because I was at my house.

Foret: Did you ever walk by the Hyatt Regency?

Knapper: No.

Foret: You never walked by the Hyatt Regency?

Knapper: I pass that way before, going on Canal Street.

Foret: You did pass by the Hyatt Regency occasionally?

Knapper: A good little while back.

Foret: You used to walk by the Hyatt Regency on the Poydras side or the Loyola side?

Knapper: On the Loyola side.

Foret: If you were standing in front of the Hyatt Regency, facing Poydras, the Superdome is to my back, okay. Canal Street is to my left, and Earhart Blvd to my right. Which way would you have to turn to get to your house?

Knapper: I have to turn to Earhardt.

Foret: You have to turn to your right?

Knapper: Yeah.

Foret: You have to turn to your right, towards Earhardt, go toward Martin Luther King?

Knapper: Yeah.

Foret: You would have to cross over a parking lot and pass the post office by the bus station?

Knapper: Yeah, to get to my house.

Foret: Did you leave that house at any time that night?

Knapper: No.

Foret: And everybody was there, and it was…I believe you

said it was about eleven people? They swear you never left that house?

Knapper: My sisters and them, we was in the room together, playing music.

Foret: About how many people?

Knapper: All of us wasn't in the room together, some was in my momma's room, kitchen.

Foret: About how many?

Knapper: Eleven or twelve.

Foret: And they can all come here and say you were there that night?

Knapper: Yeah, they can say I was there.

Foret: Now, Isaac, you realize, I'm sure, that everybody sitting here realizes that this whole case relies upon the testimony of Leroy Williams—

Isaac's attorney interrupted this line of questioning, claiming that it was argumentative.

Finally, Foret asked: Does Leroy Williams have anything against you? Have you ever done anything to Leroy Williams?

Knapper: No.

Foret: Would he have any reason to try and get you, try and get you convicted?

Again the defense attorney objected, and Foret redirected his line of questioning.

Foret: Have you ever done anything to Leroy Williams?

Knapper: No.

Foret: That would make him come here and testify against you?

Knapper: No, I ain't never done nothing.

Foret: Do you know any reason why he would come in here and lie?

The court interjected: You are asking him a question that has a thousand answers.

Foret: But you and him have never had any frictions in the past?

Knapper: No.

Foret: The uncle that was suppose(d) to go with ya'll [sic] to the country, what's his name?

Knapper: Jerry.

Foret: Jerry what?

Knapper: I don't know his last name.

Foret: He's your uncle, and you don't know his last name?

Knapper: Yeah.

Foret: Did you tell Mr. Merritt his name?

Knapper: Yeah, I told him his name was Jerry.

Foret: You told him his name was Jerry, and your uncle, but you don't know his last name?

Knapper: Momma knows his last name. He don't be around us much.

Foret: And you knew, in your own mind, that this trip to the country was coming up, right?

Knapper: Yeah, I knew.

Foret: And you would be in McComb, Mississippi, on Good Friday?

Knapper: Right.

Foret: I have nothing further.

Isaac —

When the trial began, I was a seventeen-year-old Black teenager up against a white rookie assistant district attorney, David

Paddison; a white principal investigator, John Dillman; and a white judge. This all-white team worked diligently to secure my conviction any way they could get it.

It really did not matter how we approached defending these charges because Judge Shea blocked every legal motion we presented. Regardless of the issue being raised, or whether we presented it in written form or through oral argument, all motions were denied.

By nine that evening, a mere thirteen hours after the trial started, the jury found me guilty. Who could blame them? Judge Shea threw my only hope, Clyde Merritt, out of the courtroom, all of my motions were denied, and Zibilich was so ineffective that it looked as if Detective Dillman had paid him off. But Dillman did not need to pay him off, because Judge Shea had already stacked the deck against me before the trial had even begun. The verdict was as predetermined and predictable as the fact that the sun would rise in the east the following morning.

The only people surprised by the verdict were my family. My sister Christine Lee, upon hearing the verdict, had a nervous breakdown right in the courtroom. I will never forget Judge Shea's response to my sister's pain: "Get her out of here now!" he yelled at the top of his lungs. He had no compassion, and he showed no mercy.

When the verdict was read, I crashed down in my chair at the defense table, my head in my hands. Before the guards grabbed me to haul me back to prison, I lifted my head and for a split second, my eyes locked with Judge Shea's. He had just sat back down after yelling at my distraught sister and what I saw in his eyes is etched in my mind forever. Someone once told me that the eyes are the window to the soul. At that moment, when our eyes locked, I saw into Judge Shea's soul. In his eyes I saw a man who knew he had railroaded an innocent man and would not lose a minute of sleep over it. But what he saw in my eyes was not the naïve, scared kid he had clearly hoped for. Instead, he saw determination in my eyes. Sure, there was pain and there was anger, the same anger I had embraced a few months earlier after my first beating at the hands of Dillman. I believe what he saw in me shook Judge Shea, because after our eyes locked, he looked away quickly, perhaps in hopes of denying any reality of our paths crossing again in the future.

12

ANGOLA

Isaac Knapper

Angola. Its nickname was Hell, and Hell was 18,000 acres at the end of the world. Nearly thirty square miles of prison land. If you wanted to escape, you had to either be a great swimmer or have a boat. The Louisiana State Penitentiary, Angola, lies twenty-two miles off Route 66, northwest of St. Francisville, and is surrounded by swampland and the Mississippi River on three sides. Angola is a self-contained town that is completely separate from the rest of the United States. It has its own radio station, magazine, and hospital. In fact, it has pretty much everything you need, from the time you walk through the gates till the time you die. When I was there nothing came in from the outside, and nothing left either. In fact, Angola is the only penitentiary in the U.S. that has its own zip code.

When I entered Angola, it was equipped with its own helicopters, boats, Jet Skis, four-wheel-drive trucks, and all-terrain vehicles. With all of these recreational vehicles on hand, a prisoner's chance of getting away—on foot or by swimming—were slim to none. If the vehicles didn't work, there were always horses, bloodhounds, and a large contingent of attack dogs to help track down escapees. And, obviously, you had to first get by the armed guards, who would rather shoot than chase after you.

The primary reason that prisoners tried to escape in the first place was the danger lurking *inside* those fences topped with razor wire, where many inmates were ready to kill you simply for how you looked.

This place, this hell, was where I was destined to spend the rest of my life. The day I arrived, I was one of thirty-five prisoners, aged seventeen to fifty, shackled together on the prison bus. As we and our escort from the sheriff's department approached the front gates, the complex known as Angola grew more and more massive. The bus finally stopped in front of the green-and-white gates and a big sign that greeted every new prisoner:

WELCOME TO LOUISIANA STATE PENITENTIARY
ANGOLA

Yes, sir, this was where I was about to spend the rest of my life for a crime I didn't commit. As a crossing arm lifted, an overweight guard with thin blond hair entered the bus. He introduced himself and, by his own admission, claimed to be a "redneck" and a "coon-ass." "Welcome to Angola State Penitentiary," he said sarcastically. "Some of you might have heard of this place, and for the ones of you that haven't, you're about to enter the Ponderosa. There aren't any guarantees you'll leave this place alive. If you have any enemies here, you need to tell the Freeman (the Correctional Officers) when you get to the AU [Admission Unit]—he'll see to it that you're kept separated." He motioned for the bus to move on.

When the bus stopped a second time, we were escorted off, struggling with the chains on our wrists and ankles as we walked to the AU. Once there we were unshackled, stripped naked, allowed to shower, and issued a small pile of clothes, which would be our wardrobe for the rest of our lives. Every prisoner stayed in the AU for the first week and then appeared before a board of Correctional Officers (COs), who determined his initial placement.

During the week I spent in the AU, my job was to serve food to the convicts on death row and administrative lockdown. The job seemed simple enough—slide a plate of food through a slot in front of each cell. I figured this wouldn't be a problem, and in fact, the first two deliveries went smoothly. After placing the food tray through the slot in the third cell and walking away, I heard the tray smash against the wall and fall to the floor. Food splattered everywhere, and when I turned around to see what had happened, I got my first glance of Treacherous Slim, one of the most feared men in Angola.

"You don't put that shit into my cell door," he snarled at me. "I don't eat that garbage!"

I just looked at him and then looked at the Freeman, who just turned his head and pretended not to see what had just happened. With no knowledge about the unit or Treacherous Slim, I showed no fear.

Slim then glared at me and hissed that if he could get his hands around my neck, he would choke my ass to death. I didn't know who this man was, and I didn't care. All I knew was that he had just hit a nerve, and so I screamed to the Freeman, "Let his fucking ass out of that shell!"

The Freeman shook his head, explaining that there was no way he would let that monster out. He told me I was fucking with Treacherous Slim and that was not a smart thing to do given that he had already killed more people than I could ever imagine. He was quite sure that if he let Treacherous Slim out, he would kill both of us. He implored me to just keep moving along.

Missing his point entirely, I argued, insisting that I didn't give a fuck how many people Treacherous Slim had killed, that it did not make him more of a man than I was.

"Look!" the Freeman said forcefully. "Move along and get that food out."

I thought of myself as a tough guy; so for the next four days, I threw Treacherous Slim's food through the slot, which not surprisingly sent him into a murderous rage. He would throw the tray back at me, then hurl bars of soap, or whatever else he could find. He threatened to kill me three times a day. I would fight back, knowing I was safe on the other side of the bars.

Angola had a lot of cell blocks, and the board asked questions to determine where you should be placed; they were primarily trying to find out who needed protection from whom. When I first entered Angola, I had no idea that it was considered to be the bloodiest prison in the country, a place where crimes like rape, murder, and beatings were daily occurrences. Unaware of Angola's reputation, I told the board that I didn't need any damn protection, and that even if I did, they couldn't protect me anyway. They assigned me, and eleven of the guys from the bus, to cell block A. I learned later that this was the most dangerous, tense, and volatile cell block of them all.

Like all things new, Angola just seemed strange to me. It looked like something out of a Roman prison movie. Any time men needed to move from one point to another, they were put into lines—chow line, work line, lines for everything. Even the lines in the field (every new convict was assigned to the field unless he was physically unable to work and had a medical excuse) were created to keep the convicts separated and easier to watch by the Freeman. Thirty-one men and I, all from the same cell block, were assigned to work line seven.

I was in prison a full year before I learned that they had assigned me to A block as punishment. When I arrived at Angola, I was full of anger—looking, as I was, at a life sentence—so I guess they thought I'd fit right in with the convicts in the most violent cell block, which was populated by ruthless predators, wolves, and rapists. Fortunately, I had been the best fighter at the parish prison, and the respect this generated gave me at least some protection.

Angola locks up its prisoners longer than any other prison on earth. There are an estimated four hundred and twenty-five men there, ranging in ages from fifty-two to eighty-six, who have been imprisoned for longer than thirty years. Since very few convicts ever leave, Angola has to be huge, and the place features more than eighty separate units, each with a distinct personality and role within the prison. The main prison and most popular unit is known as the "big yard." While each unit has its own visiting rooms, athletic facilities, and "dungeons" (punishment cells or "holes"), the big yard was known for housing the best athletes and equipment. More than twelve hundred inmates live there.

The main prison had several working cell blocks, including A, B, C, and D blocks (with D block serving as the dungeon).

Units within these blocks have inviting names like Oak, Pine, Walnut, and Hickory. The main prison also housed the "Mag" unit, which, in the eighties, was designed as a protection unit where men were housed if they feared an attack from another inmate. Unfortunately, in reality, it was impossible to protect prisoners from attack in Angola.

There were more than six thousand prisoners held in Angola—men who were going to become my new friends, men with whom I would be spending the rest of my life. They had names like Mose Murry, Hog-Head, Bobby Hop, Bedfa, Mountain Duck, and Treacherous Slim, and some of them were serving three or four life sentences. In the yard you'd hear guys say that they were in for three hundred years rather than three life sentences—it didn't sound quite as long.

Many of these guys are now gone, killed in Angola by other convicts or felled by disease. Whatever the cause, very few inmates make it out alive. In fact, for most men in Angola, life is on the line every day. There are no small disagreements and for any dispute, you can pay with your life.

I soon learned that in Angola a weapon was your ID card—and the weapon of choice was a knife. Without a knife or two, you had no identity and your days were numbered. When I first arrived, my brother-in-law, Willie—who was already serving a 198-year sentence—sent me a welcome surprise: two knives tucked away in a food cart driven by two other convicts. With these two knives in my possession, I felt powerful. Early in my stay, there were times that I felt like killing someone simply to justify being sentenced for a murder I didn't commit.

At seventeen, I was a tough kid, and I soon became friends with one of Angola's most dangerous and notorious convicts—Mose Murry. Most people called him "Graveyard," and he was a bundle of rage. If he noticed someone looking in his direction, he'd turn his head and look the other way. If the guy was still looking in his direction when he looked back, he would immediately order the guy to get his knife and meet him in the H, a long space between cell blocks that served as a knife-fighting ring. If the convict didn't have a knife, Graveyard would give him one of his own.

Graveyard was the first convict I noticed walking around with a shoestring hanging out of his pocket. Sometimes he'd have a second one hanging over his shoulder. In the rec yard one day, I asked him what was up with the shoestrings. He had taken me under his wing—a process known as "schooling a young fish to the penitentiary rules and laws of the land"—and he just said, "Let's take a walk, young blood."

I quickly learned that the shoestring is used in a knife fight. When two convicts have a disagreement over something serious, they get another inmate to tie their wrists together. The two men are then handed their knives, and most of the time, someone dies. This was called separating the inmates from the convicts, the boys from the men. When you see a convict on the compound with a shoestring showing, he's letting you know that he is "about it."

I had a good friend in Angola named Derrick Robinson, or D-Monster. He was twenty, and Graveyard had taken him under his wing too—he called us his two sons because we reminded him of himself when he first entered Angola in 1962. Graveyard taught us the laws of the prison, and the shoestring was one of our lessons—he would tie our wrists together and then give us rulers so we could learn how to "string-up" for a knife fight without actually hurting each other.

In Angola there were rules, and then there were laws. The rules, which were made by the warden and enforced by the correctional officers, were fairly uniform throughout the U.S. prison system. The laws, on the other hand, were created by the inmates themselves, and the number-one law was to do whatever it took to survive. There were no lawyers or judges. If you got into trouble with a Freeman or another convict, convict counselors were appointed to represent you, or you could represent yourself in a disciplinary hearing.

Killing was a monthly occurrence, and there was no jury or court to determine guilt or innocence. If you injured or killed another convict, you were placed on administrative lockdown in a tiny one-man cell for about ten days. From there you would go to either Camp J or CCR (Close Cell Restricted), the extended lockdown unit, to wait for your new indictment. At that point, you might as well get comfortable, because it could take up to three years before they would even consider sending you back to the general population. Once you go into extended lockdown, you're given another life sentence. Most convicts don't care; they're already resigned to dying there.

Camp J and CCR were similar—one-man cells with a metal bed about two feet wide and six feet long covered with a very thin mattress. The worst thing about the cell was that the toilet was right in the corner, wide open. There was no privacy in Angola because of the ever-present threat of violence.

The working cell blocks were different. For example, my cell in Camp A was #8, a 10-by-8-foot cell with two bunks and a front door that had one-and-a-half-inch bars all the way across. The only entertainment was provided by the TVs attached to the walls in the walkway outside the cells. To watch a show, I'd stand in the front of the cell and look through the bars.

All the working cell blocks came with a cellie (another convict), whom you didn't know but learned to adjust to. You had to be extremely careful, because you never knew who your cellie was and what he was capable of doing. In Angola, every man thought differently, and every man was trying to survive while surrounded by six thousand other inmates.

Camp F was a "trustee camp," home to prisoners who had been in Angola long enough and behaved well enough to earn the trust of the corrections officers and the warden. Even though they were still serving life sentences, they had a certain degree of freedom within the confines of the prison. Camp F was also home to the prison's electric chair, at least until the state switched to lethal injection. Every time someone was executed in the electric chair, the camp lights would go out for thirty seconds.

Many camps served multiple purposes. For example, Camp

H had a dormitory, a trustee unit, and a twenty-four-hour extended lockdown, while Camp D was called the home of the "wings," or the "bird camp," nicknames for Eagle Unit, a protection unit, Falcon, a big strike or general population unit, and Hawk, an extended lockdown unit. In extended lockdown, only one convict at a time was allowed out of his cell for forty-five minutes a day. During that time he could walk inside or go to the rec yard, a twenty-four-foot-square dog pen designed to allow inmates to walk in a circle.

While many different camps had a lockdown unit, Camp J's extended lockdown unit was infamous as the most unsafe, godforsaken unit in all of Angola. It was there that the "worst of the worst" prisoners were held, for anything from killing another man to throwing feces in a CO's face.

CCR was an extended-lockdown unit reserved for prisoners who were considered capable of killing in the blink of an eye and were thus a security risk. One of the more renowned prisoners in CCR was a man called Woodfox, who had been on lockdown for thirty-nine years for allegedly killing a correctional lieutenant. He never rejoined the general population, which was hard to understand since others who had killed two or even three fellow prisoners would stay on lockdown for three years and then be allowed to return to the general population saddled with another life sentence. It seemed as if an officer's life was more valuable than the lives of several inmates.

The prison guards in Angola doubled as the body-removal squad. When a man was killed or died from an illness, the guards would drag the body out in a black bag and take it to the in-house morgue, where it would remain until a family member claimed it. Unclaimed bodies were buried at Point Lookout, Angola's cemetery; convicts conducted their own services for the deceased.

When new convicts first arrived, they were sent to the fields to work. All of the prison's food was grown and picked in the fields, and the work there—with long hours in the pounding heat—was considered "cruel and unusual punishment" by the inmates. Any inmate who wanted to graduate to a job on the compound needed to complete ninety days in the fields without a write-up or incident report. It was nearly impossible to complete the ninety days. If the field foreman didn't like you, he might wait until you were at day eighty-nine and then issue you an incident report, which meant your ninety days started all over again.

I saw men take a knife and cut a finger off just to get light-duty status so they wouldn't have to work in the fields. Another common ploy was to pour battery acid on top of your foot and let it burn a silver-dollar-size hole straight through. This would get a prisoner out of the fields, but would also result in a disciplinary report. It took me eleven years to complete my ninety days of fieldwork without an incident report!

The doctor at Angola was nicknamed Pink Paper Pete, because no matter what problem or ailment you had, he would always give you two Tylenols and a "pink paper," or disciplinary report. The COs often used the same doctor, and in one instance, a lieutenant who hadn't been feeling well paid a visit to Pink Paper Pete, the doctor who duly sent him off with a clean bill of health and two Tylenols. The CO turned, took three steps to leave the office, and fell dead on the floor.

After three or four weeks in Angola, I met with eleven of the inmates I had arrived with to discuss protecting ourselves from being killed or—even worse—getting raped by other convicts. I had two knives, but none of the others had any, and when I offered to give them one of my knives, no one would take it. We made a pact at the meeting to stick together and kill anyone who tried to fuck with any one of us. We would stand united, side by side, no matter what happened. At that point, I had a life sentence, two knives, and a really bad attitude about life in general, and I took it upon myself to be the leader of the pack.

The very next day, a convict named Boger Lee sat on the floor in front of my cell. He was visiting to warn me that there were rumors around about the "pretty boys" I had come in with. Word had spread that I was the leader of the pack, and that if anyone looked at me the wrong way, I would kill him. He shared that no one would fuck with me, but the rest of my group was considered fresh meat.

"I'm ready for anything they bring," I assured Lee. "You have to bring ass to get ass. They know not to fuck with me!" I yelled.

"Nap, you're right," Lee said, "but they'll make a move on your friends, and I don't know if you're aware of this cell block, but there are some sick motherfuckers here, and they're very dangerous."

"You go back and let them freaks know that I will die or kill, whichever comes first, before I turn my back and let my friends get raped," I told him. "We all made vows that we'll help each other as long as we're in this pen. So go and let them fags know I said we're not looking for trouble, but we ain't running, either. I don't have anything to lose."

Later in the day, I exchanged small talk in the yard with my brother-in-law, Willie. He came to the fence and asked how things were going. He said he was checking up on me because he had heard rumors that my friends' manhood would be tested. I assured him I was fine and didn't feel threatened. He encouraged me to watch my back because that night was movie night. When the lights were turned off and it was pitch dark, a lot of killing took place, he told me. He wanted to make sure I brought my knives.

The theater was the gym, and we called it "The Wall." It was a dangerous place and the scene of so many killings that they eventually stopped showing movies there and just put TVs in the cell-block hallways. I was ready for anything that night, but nothing happened. In fact, that day ended up being more memorable for another reason—the first visit from my momma. From that day forward she rarely missed a weekly visit during the fourteen years I was in Angola, despite the two-hour drive from her home in New Orleans.

I was in the field working and keeping a close eye on the

convicts in my area when I saw a white truck drive up. The Freeman called my name and I jumped into the back of the pickup, happy to be out of the field for the rest of the day and even more excited for my first contact visit.

"Oh, baby!" Momma cried the instant she laid eyes on me. "Are you all right?" she asked as she gave me a tight hug. "Here," she said, pushing me back. "Let me get a good look at you. Are you all right? Baby, I'm so worried about you!"

"Momma, please don't cry. And don't worry about me," I assured her. "Everything will be all right. Besides, I have your blood and your strength, and I'm strong and very tough, just like you, Momma."

"Oh, baby," she cried. "This is a terrible place. They kill people and hurt them."

"Momma, please always remember one thing," I told her. "You raised me to be a man, and that's just what I am. If they put me in a cage with a dog, I'll become a tiger. Whatever I have to do to survive, I'll do it; and if I have to kill to protect my manhood, I will." I was talking tough, and in the end it would turn out to be true. "They'll get more than they bring to the table with me," I added. I told her not to worry and gave her another hug. "I love you, Momma," I said, knowing deep down that my life at Angola would be rough. I dreaded the thought that she might come one day and get the bad news she feared—that another inmate had killed me.

Momma asked if I had my Bible and I lied that I did. She asked if I was reading it every day. I lied again, telling her I was but knowing there wasn't time for praying around here when I was busy just trying to survive. This was something I couldn't tell her, because I didn't want her to be scared any more than she already was. I just kept the tough face on and never let her know any different.

"Okay, baby," she said. "I just love you so much." She couldn't stop crying.

Three-thirty came around fast, signaling the end of our visit. I went back to A block, thinking about the visit and the look in my mother's eyes. I had just turned seventeen and I knew I would be in Angola for the rest of my life, and certainly for the rest of Momma's life.

The first killing I witnessed was in the chow hall. Farris was built like the famous bodybuilder Charles Atlas, and he was always pushing his weight around. On this day, he was pushing the food cart for the noon lunch typically served in our cells. As he pulled up to each cell, we would dip our cups through the bars into a container of juice. That day he decided to urinate into the juice bucket and tell some of the convicts not to drink it. He made a fatal mistake in not sharing this news with Big Duck, who weighed 260 pounds but wasn't all that tough. Truth be told, he didn't need to be tough, because he was one of those inmates who would kill at the drop of a hat, literally. If he had a problem with anyone, he would just kill him.

As Duck was about to fill his cup with juice, his friend in the suite next door, Mose, shared the news. My cell was on the other side of Duck's, so I had a ringside seat to the confrontation.

"Why did you piss in the juice?" Big Duck growled at Farris. "You trying to make me drink your piss?"

Farris, looking a bit shocked that Big Duck knew, didn't back down. "That's right," he snarled back. "If I didn't want you to drink my piss, I would have told you about it."

"Oh yeah?" Big Duck exploded. "I tell you what, nigga! When they call chow, meet me in the mess hall and bring your iron with you!"

Farris shook his head and laughed. As he walked away, he looked back and said, "Yeah, yeah. I'll be there!"

Everybody arrived at the mess hall that evening ready to see Duck and Farris "sling iron" or knife fight. We all brought our own blades in case we were jumped while the fighting happened. Big Duck was ready, but Farris didn't show, which further aggravated Duck. At that point, he was so far gone that he was looking for anything or anybody to vent his anger on. As he looked around, wild-eyed, he spotted Farris's two gal-boys, Pencil and Black Girl. Big Duck approached the table where they were eating and stabbed Pencil right through the heart with a sixteen-inch knife. Pencil was dead before he hit the floor, while Black Girl took off running. Duck didn't give chase—he wasn't exactly built for speed.

Duck's life sentences were adding up—he came with one, got the second for killing another convict, and got his third for killing Pencil. I've always wondered about someone who had more than one life sentence; if they died and were reborn, would they have to come back to Angola as a baby? Big Duck stayed on lockdown for three years before being released back into the general population.

Farris lived for two more years in protective custody and, after fifteen years in Angola, was released while Big Duck was still in lockdown. Farris was lucky to stay alive until his discharge, but four months later, he was found dead with a bullet in his head in the St. Bernard housing projects. Once again, he must have pissed somebody off.

I was overwhelmed by the hellish environment and surrounded by violence and murder, and so it was just a matter of time before I made my first mistake. It happened in the fields where I was working on my ninety days without a write-up. I was about to get "mud-ass deep" waiting for my first assignment.

Each cell block had its own line of eighty to a hundred convicts assigned to work in the fields. Each line had a "Head-Land," who was in charge of assigning the other convicts to a small area of dirt where they would work for the rest of the day. The Head-Land approached each convict individually and used his shovel to mark the inmate's work area in the dirt.

When my Head-Land, Darrell, stood in front of me and marked my spot, I felt pissed off.

"Nigga, you don't tell me where to work," I snapped.

Darrell stopped, shocked by my attitude. "Look, Red. You don't need to get on me about this shit. If you don't want to work, just throw the fucking shovel down and ride out." He turned and walked to the next spot.

"If I ride out," I spoke without thinking, "it's going to be for putting this shovel up your big ass!"

I was young and full of rage, sentenced to life in Angola for a murder I didn't commit. Everybody around me was violent, and though this sounds crazy now, I wanted to be just like them. I wanted to kill someone—or two or three. In fact, I needed to kill someone to have a big name. I was sure I'd never walk free again—everyone around me was serving the same life sentence, and they'd been there for twenty-five, thirty, even thirty-five years. I figured I was no different.

I was angry and full of hate, and since I had just run my mouth, I now had to back it up. While he was marking the next spot, I flew at him, whacking the back of his head with a shovel. Part of his head separated from the rest. I was trying to kill him. I really wanted him to die, and if a guard on horseback hadn't been there, he would have been dead. The guard fired a round of ammo into the ground at my feet, warning me to step back and drop the shovel. Knowing the next round would be meant for me instead of the dirt, I did both. And then I rode out, just as Darrell had suggested.

Darrell was never the same after I attacked him, and three years later we saw each other again. The officers wanted him to press charges against me, but he refused. Only "rats" pressed charges against another convict, and Darrell was not a rat. Refusing to press charges was considered "keeping it gangster." Even if Darrell had considered retaliation for my assault, he couldn't have done it, because he was now confined to a wheelchair. He told me that he had been in a coma for about six months, and that when he awoke, he had lost his equilibrium. Two years after that conversation, he died.

To this day I hate myself for my immature actions toward Darrell. I also realize now that I was an innocent kid thrust into a deadly prison—for life. I was seeing so much violence and hatred toward other men, and I was becoming a product of my environment. I quickly learned that in Angola, death was a regular part of life.

After the assault on Darrell, I was sent to lockdown in Camp J, where the worst of the worst were held. When I first got there, the warden allowed each of us an hour a day to walk around in a pen. They had just taken away the hour hall walk because the inmates would fight through the bars—it was called bar fighting.

The prison cells in Camp J all faced a long hallway, and throughout the day a single inmate would be allowed out of his cell to walk the hallway for an hour. Of course, the guy who was on the hall walk would soon try to get even with the guy with whom he had been bar fighting. One common tactic was for the convict in lockdown to get some gas from a trustee who came to clean the lockdown unit. Then, during his hall walk, the inmate would walk by a cell, throw the gas in, and quickly follow it with a lit match.

"Shitting him down" was another common fighting technique. An inmate would save his shit in an ice cream cup—some guys would save ten, twenty, or even more cups of human waste, which might be two or three months old when it was finally flung into a cell during a convict's hallway walk. Human waste, in fact, was often an important weapon at Camp J—some convicts would even try to buy it from you. They'd use it to make homemade darts with feces on the tip. Human feces are full of bacteria, so if you got hit by one of those darts, you not only lost your dignity but were assured of a roaring infection.

On lockdown, I lived in cell nine, and my friend Michael Johnson was in cell ten. It helped to have a friend nearby. The summer heat was scorching, and to make matters even worse, the redneck guards would turn the heat on to make us as miserable as possible. In the winter the Deep South gets cold, and the guards would turn the air conditioning on so we would freeze our asses off. Physical torment was a way of life in Camp J.

To fight the heat, we would stop up the toilets so the water would overflow onto the floor. Once it was good and flooded, we would get naked and lie on the wet, cool floor. One day, while in this very position, I heard the Freeman's keys rattle. I jumped up and grabbed my peeper—a piece of mirror on the tip of my toothbrush—to see who was coming. I watched as the chaplain slowly walked past each cell, then stopped in front of mine.

The only reason the chaplain would visit anyone in Camp J was to deliver bad news. As he stood in front of my cell, fear crept over me. I didn't want to hear anything he had to say. I came as close to the bars as possible and began to scream at him, "Get away from my cell!"

My friend Michael started screaming with me. "You heard him," he shouted. "Get the fuck away from his cell, mother-fucker."

The preacher said, with a cool demeanor, "I'm sorry. Your brother, Larry Lee, was killed in a car accident. His car plunged off a bridge into a river. He drowned. I've arranged for you to make a call home to your family." In that moment, the hammer fell and the room caved in. All I could think about was what Momma must be going through as her three sons were taken from her, one by one. I had to keep reminding myself that I needed to hold in my tears, that tough guys don't cry. That painful night passed very slowly.

When the morning came, Momma was there to visit me. This was her first visit with me in lockdown, so we were sitting on different sides of the cage with no physical contact. I was shackled at my feet with a chain around my waist to keep my handcuffs in place. Momma was smoking cigarettes, something I had never seen her do. With her head in her arms, she sobbed very hard and when she finally looked up at me, my heart skipped a beat. It felt as though it had been ripped out of my chest.

I wanted to reach out to her, to hold her, to comfort her, to kiss her tears away. The one person I loved more than anyone was tormented, and I couldn't even hold her hands. I was a man now at nineteen, and I needed to embrace my mother until her pain went away. The prison system had no compassion, no kindness. It was as cold as the North Pole in winter. Anger began to explode through my veins, held back by the tight chains that bound me.

"Momma, please don't cry," I pleaded. "Why are you smoking? I've never seen you smoke before."

"Oh, son," she cried. "I don't know why. I just don't know why I've lost all my sons. Larry is dead now. They put you in here for life, and Corneal is waiting to be sentenced to life for the same reason. What have I done that is so wrong? I tried so hard for all my children." She wept uncontrollably.

"Momma," I said. "I won't be here for the rest of my life. And Corneal won't either. I promise you that, Momma." I was trying to say all the right things, but without the compassionate hug, the words seemed hollow.

Through the cage, I watched helplessly as my mother broke down. She just couldn't get ahold of herself. Muscles of steel, strength of a giant, fast as lightning—it didn't matter, because now I, too, was crying. If I could just make all of this go away. But I couldn't.

Momma talked to the warden about allowing me to be released for the funeral, but her pleas were in vain—I was considered a security risk. The visit ended as fast as it had begun. I was in agony as I watched my mother leave, alone. The pressure built like a boiling teakettle as I struggled back to my cell. I felt so helpless. The one time my mother needed me the most, I had let her down. My mother's whole life was dedicated to her family—especially to me. I didn't want to hear the "it will be all right" or "be strong" lines—it wasn't going to be okay, and I suddenly didn't feel tough at all.

When the Freeman asked me what was wrong, I cussed him out and got just want I wanted, but not what I needed—a transfer to solitary confinement. Life was too heavy a burden for me to handle right then, and I wasn't strong enough to handle this much frustration. As I sat holding my head in my hands, I realized my hair was falling out in globs.

Everyone tried to explain why this was happening to me, but without God in my life, I could never understand any of the explanations. The one explanation that made the most sense to me was that "the Lord was testing me." I was reaching the end of my rope—I needed something good to happen to me, and eventually it did. The frustrated energy that was building up motivated me to start boxing. My stubbornness almost got in the way of this opportunity.

After a year in lockdown, Major Tears from Camp A paid me a visit. He wanted to know if I would be interested in boxing on the prison team. Normally I would have jumped at this opportunity, but I was still angry at the world and didn't want to listen.

When he approached my cell and asked if I was Nap, I just sat there on the bed staring at him. He introduced himself as Major Tears from Camp A and asked if I knew D-Man, Derrick Robertson. This caught my attention, because D-Man was one of my best friends, and I had heard he was in Camp A. I got up and walked to the front of my cell and said, "Yes, I know D-Man. Why?"

Major Tears explained that D-Man claimed I was a good fighter and that he was looking for a good boxer. Then he asked, "Can you fight?"

"Yes, I can fight," I replied, but then added, "I'm not interested in boxing for anyone."

"D-Man told me that you were the guy I'm looking for," he said. "I decided to come and take a look for myself. I'm looking for someone to go up against a bad-ass middleweight named Lionel Russell. D-man said that you can beat Lionel."

I told him again that I wasn't interested, and by that point, I was getting irritated. But Major Tears was a boxing fanatic, and he wasn't going to give up so easily. He was prepared to offer anything in his power to persuade me to become his boxer.

"I can get you out of here," he said. "I can get you off lockdown today and bring you to Camp A. All you have to do is say yes."

My heart skipped a beat. Boxing must be a big deal in this place, I thought. Then I realized that if I let this guy get me off lockdown, he'd think he owned me. I couldn't do it. I refused, telling him I would wait on the review board. As bad as I wanted to get off lockdown and box, I didn't want anything held over my head.

He just looked at me. "Are you crazy?" he asked. "You could be here another year."

"So be it," I said, and sat back down on my bunk. I could understand why he thought I was crazy—no man in his right mind would stay on lockdown in Camp J. He left, but he returned six months later and asked me again. And once again, I refused. Then, after sixteen months in lockdown, my time was finally up, and the review board sent me back to a cell block—they apparently thought I was still too wild to live in the general population. This time, however, I accepted Major Tears's offer.

Boxing was a very important sport at Angola. So much so that each area had its own boxing team, and they all competed against each other. When the boxers weren't fighting each other, they were going up against convicts from other penitentiaries across the state. Because Angola was the largest prison, other smaller ones sent their boxers to Angola for the big tournaments. Only one person at a time can hold the Department of Corrections Title in their weight division, and during my time in Angola I held titles in two different weight classes, 165 pounds and, later, 178 pounds. In fact, once I started boxing, I was the champion of the penitentiary for nine years straight!

When I returned to cell block A, I was faced with a very shocking reality. My absence had opened the door for the predators to go after my friends. The eleven men I had been protecting had all been raped while I was in lockdown—they had been turned into gal-boys, even dressing and acting the part.

The only good thing about going back to A-block was that my new cellie was a man named Frank who had grown up in the Melpomene Housing Projects with me. He was a real friend at a time when I desperately needed a friend, considering that I had just lost eleven of them to the predators of A-block.

Being back on A-block also meant returning to hard labor in the fields. Just two weeks out, I was working the fields alongside Frank when an argument broke out between me and two other guys. In the fields a simple argument could easily turn deadly. However, the thought of going back on lockdown didn't bother me a bit. On the way back to the block for lunch, I told Frank how pissed off I was at these two guys, and I made it clear that after I made a phone call home to my family, "it was going down."

"Nap," Frank said, "let me take care of this problem."

"No way," I said. "I've got to handle this myself."

Again he tried to explain. "You just got off lockdown. I can do this, and if anything happens, you won't have to go back on lockdown."

Despite my protests, Frank did take care of it. On my way back to the work line, I heard yelling, as though someone was getting shanked. I turned to make sure Frank was all right, and to my surprise, he was standing over the two guys I had intended on sticking myself. Frank had taken it upon himself to take care of the problem. He didn't kill them, but he did some serious damage. He was sent to Camp J lockdown for three years.

After a few months on A-block, I was moved again to a new location: Camp A cell block, line 21. Moving to a new location was like arriving at the penitentiary for the first time all over again. You have to establish and prove yourself again.

In Camp A, I met up with Badeda, an older guy I knew from the Big Yard. When I arrived he had been in Angola for about thirty years and was pretty content with his prison routine. Most of his time was spent strolling the yard and feeding stray cats. Badeda was like many of the older convicts who had issues with the younger generation of inmates, complaining that they lacked respect for the older convicts who had already paid their dues.

This tension came to a head one day when Badeda learned

that one of his cats had been injured. While Badeda was resting in his cell, a young inmate had apparently drop-kicked the cat to see how far he could launch it. The cat flew about fifteen feet in the air and subsequently walked with a permanent limp. When Badeda noticed the limp and asked what had happened, he learned that the youngster had kicked the cat. Later that day, Badeda sneaked up behind the guy and stabbed him repeatedly. Needless to say, the young guy died.

This kind of violence was reality, the norm for all units in Angola, but especially Camp A. Sometimes the victims brought the violence on themselves. Big John was a six-foot-five, 250-pound soft white guy who claimed to be connected to the mafia in the South. He and his codefendants, who were also in the so-called Dixie Mafia, had been sentenced to life sentences.

Big John leaned toward gal-boys in the absence of women, and his one big mistake was fooling with a gal-boy who was already taken. Papa wasn't big or bad, but when pushed he became violent and vicious. Big John fell in love with Papa's gal-boy and figured he would just talk to Papa about it and everything would be okay. The talk didn't go well. Papa picked up a curl bar from the weight pile and beat Big John to death with it. Papa got another life sentence, and the beat went on.

The convicts weren't the only victims at Angola—the officers also suffered from being institutionalized. Many of the guards who worked at Angola were actually born and raised there. Part of the 18,000 acres is an area called B-land, where officers can live and raise their families just outside the prison walls while still technically remaining on the grounds. It was not unusual for convicts to watch some of the children born and raised on Angola become officers when they grew up.

After two years at Angola, I witnessed a convict offer a CO two hundred dollars to open another young inmate's cell in the middle of the night so the convict could rape him. The request wasn't surprising, but the CO simply responded, "I don't want your money. I want the young boy when you're through." When the convict refused to share his prey with the CO and threatened to take his request and the two hundred dollars to another CO on the next shift, the CO reluctantly agreed to take the money and not participate in the sexual abuse.

While serving my sentence in Angola, I wanted and needed a reputation that protected me from the predators that were part of my everyday life. When I first arrived at age seventeen, I was almost literally a sheep among wolves. I don't expect anyone to understand what it means or feels like to wake up every morning and worry that it could very well be your last day on earth; and this worry wasn't based on rumor or simple fear, but rather on the actual observation, over and over again, of men being carried out of prison in body bags.

The impact that being surrounded by death had on my young mind cannot be overstated. I believed that I needed to create an image, a reputation that would protect me from taking a life based on how dangerous others perceived me to be. I am not proud of the image I created for myself, but it did accomplish two things: first, it prevented me from ever killing anyone; and second, it protected an innocent, naïve seventeen-year-old kid from being killed in the most violent prison in America.

Mose Murry, a.k.a. "Graveyard," my mentor during my early years in Angola, understood my dilemma perfectly: I needed a reputation, and in my limited experience that meant killing someone. But in my heart, I knew that killing was wrong. In my mind, in order to survive, I was willing to do that wrong, and Graveyard knew it.

"Look, Nap, I know you're itching to make a name for yourself," he said, "but I want you to listen to what I'm about to tell you." I listened attentively.

"We both know that no one spends any time at Angola without first being tested or tried. It happens to everyone, and when it happens to you, I want you to be ready." He paused for effect. "Now, because you have a boxing background, you don't need to kill anyone—you can just knock them out and blind them."

One of the first things I learned in Angola was that a fight

rarely ended unless one man killed the other. If they both survived, the one who had lost the fight would wait for the perfect
time, sometimes days later, to surprise the victor and stab him
to death. Graveyard knew this, and he gave me some smart
advice. "If you're not going to blind them, then you'd better kill
them, because they will come back and try to kill you in order
to salvage their reputation." I sat and took it all in, prepared to
do whatever he told me to do in order to keep the predators at
bay in Angola.

"Look, Nap," Graveyard added. "It isn't like I'm telling you
to go out to the yard or to Camp A and start a bunch of fights
and blind people—I'm not saying that. I'm saying that when
you're forced to fight, you end it without getting killed or killing
anyone."

One of the ways to protect yourself in prison if you weren't
involved in a formal gang was to never walk alone. Guys always
had two or three close friends to whom they swore allegiance,
and each group was widely known throughout the system. If
you found yourself in a disagreement with one man, it would
often escalate and involve the two or three friends who were
part of his small group. For much of my time in Angola, my
group consisted of Michael Johnson, D-Monster, and myself. If
you had an issue with one of us, you had an issue with all of us.

One day, I came upon a bully who had gotten into it with
D-Monster, and I knew I had to act. While the guy was brushing
his teeth, I quickly approached him and knocked him out with
a quick left and then a right. Within fifteen minutes, covered in
the guy's blood, I was taken to the dungeon. I spent six months
in solitary but was never charged with assault. The man lived, as
did I, which was as much a part of the rationale for the assault
as the protection of my friends.

During my fourteen years in Angola, I was involved in five
other altercations. I am mortified and ashamed of what I did to
survive and to protect my friends, but I never killed anyone, and
in a place with so much killing, that matters.

13

Picking up the Pieces

Amy Banks

In 1979, while my family was at my father's funeral, well-intentioned friends removed all of his clothing from the house. When we returned home the house was filled with people and casseroles but devoid of any physical evidence of his existence. My siblings and I had no chance to pick out an oversized shirt or sweater that might still smell of his familiar pipe tobacco—a little sensory comfort for the worst nights of grief and despair. A small eight-by-ten portrait painted by a local artist and hung in the kitchen was about all of him that remained. And even here my father's left shoulder was inexplicably unfinished—it stood out as a hazy, undefined, gray mass that lacked the fine striped detail of the rest of his suit coat, almost as though he were disappearing in front of our eyes. I can see now that his "disappearance" from the house was part of a larger traumatic reaction meant to protect my family from the horror of the murder. It backfired.

The vacuum it created only amplified my longing. I was desperate to find him and spent many afternoons at the cemetery—the only place where I felt sure he existed. The visits were tormenting. My family was as nonreligious as they came, which meant that I couldn't even fall back on the belief that my father was safely in some heaven where guns and hate don't exist. To me, he was simply locked in a steel coffin, cemented inside a vault and buried under a ton of dirt. When the feeling of claustrophobia made it impossible to breathe, I would leave.

Family friends did their best to support us, but the message was clear: Our job was to build lives that consciously honored our father's memory, and through the years we did this as best we could. Old New England stoicism was expected at home, and it often seemed that his memory had disappeared with his clothes. There were exceptions. My mother always referenced him to mark an important milestone or accomplishment. She honored my graduation from high school, college, and medical school with a card reminding me of Dad's intellectual gifts and how much he would have loved celebrating this success with me. Each year on the anniversary of his murder, she would send each of us bright spring flowers with a moving note honoring Dad's legacy and emphasizing how proud he would have been of each of us. The silence during the rest of the year fed a ravenous craving for any mention of his life, his work, his love. My mother died long before I had the awareness to ask where my father lived inside her all of those lonely years.

Nancy and my father had only eight years together. The vanishing act made keeping her few memories of him alive more difficult. For the five days between Dad's death and his funeral she was sent to friends' houses, then "protected" from the funeral by staying at home with a beloved family friend, Norma, who adored her. By the time Nancy was twelve, she had filled the void with an impressive obsession with the very visible stories of John and Robert Kennedy, two fathers who had also been gunned down in the prime of their lives. I suspect that the images of the Kennedy family's grace and grief resonated deeply with her own undefined ache; the picture of Robert Kennedy on the floor of the Ambassador Hotel, blood pooling around his head, providing a visual to a murder only whispered about in her own family. Once when I was home from college, she shared a dream with me that she had been walking through the Bangor Mall with Robert Kennedy. It was so sweet and totally heartbreaking.

A scholarship was set up at the university in my father's name and awarded each year to a distinguished young scholar of Maine history. For the first couple of years our whole family attended the ceremony, but over time, as Kate, Phil, and I grew older and moved farther away from Maine, my mother and

Nancy would attend alone. For Nancy, this was the one day each year on which her father was celebrated openly.

Months after my father's murder, a New Orleans law firm reached out to my mother to discuss a lawsuit against the Hyatt Regency Hotel. They arrived at our split-level ranch home in Brewer with smooth, Southern drawls and a stack of police reports documenting extensive criminal activity around the hotel since its opening in 1976, proof that the Hyatt was well aware of the grave danger that the location posed to their guests. We had naïvely created a story for ourselves that the assault on my father and John had been an extremely rare, unlikely event, and so we were shocked by the Hyatt Regency's apparent carelessness. The murder may have been a one-in-a-million event, but it also could have been prevented.

The civil lawsuit, *Banks v. Hyatt,* sought monetary damages for the wrongful death of my father, but just as important, the case was an attempt to force the hotel to take responsibility for shoddy security practices. The Hyatt refused to settle out of court, betting that no jury would find them responsible for the death of a tourist outside their hotel doors. In the spring of 1981, with no idea what to expect, my family boarded a plane bound for New Orleans to attend the David vs. Goliath trial that we assumed we had little chance of winning. There was no precedent in hotel security law on which to base our case, and the Hyatt had endless corporate resources and a clear incentive to protect their image at all cost.

The trial lasted a full week, five times longer than it had taken to convict Isaac Knapper of murder. From the moment the judge called the room to order, the proceedings were revolting. My family was seated in the first bench immediately behind the defense table, much too close to the slick Hyatt lawyers. They were grotesquely friendly and flirtatious with my mother—I can only assume it was a premeditated attempt on their part to seem less corporate and more humane. The Hyatt's argument was simple: My father's murder was a tragic accident, but it was also my father's fault for walking around a dangerous city after dark. Around the middle of the week, after the forensic details of the case were laid out for the jury, each member of my family was called to the witness stand and questioned about the impact of our father's death. Even ten-year-old Nancy swore to tell the truth, the whole truth, and nothing but the truth about her father, her sweet towhead barely poking above the dark mahogany witness stand. When Kate attempted to share her close relationship with Dad, she simply wept. In the recap of our family testimony at the end of the day, our lawyers thought her honest display of emotion was good for the jurors to see. As the trial went on, it was hard not to feel like a pawn in a much larger game over which we had little control.

As the week progressed, I became preoccupied by a desire to see the exact spot on which my father had been killed. By mid-week the thought was starting to drive me crazy, so I decided, during a lunch break, to walk the few blocks to the crime scene, dragging Nancy along with me. The lawyers had spent half a day describing the specific location of my father's body in relation to the entrance to the hotel, with his feet lying just four feet from the door and his body resting under the awning that hung over the sidewalk. As Nancy and I retraced our dad's footsteps down Loyola Avenue toward the hotel, I was overcome with an unsettling spacey numbness. I stood staring at the spot, trying to imagine my father's large body helplessly sprawled over the sidewalk, the elements having long ago washed away the blood that had pooled around his head. As we walked back to the courthouse, the numbness turned into a cavernous aching pit in my torso as the reality sank in: I was not going to find my father here in New Orleans. He was never coming back.

Closing arguments finished early on Friday, and we were all ushered outside the courtroom to await the verdict. The adults made small talk that did nothing to cut the palpable tension. Bodies fidgeted on benches and paced the hallways for two hours while the case was debated. There was no distraction from the nervousness—every echoing footstep pounded into my head like Chinese water torture.

The jurors seemed serious and tense as they filed back into the courtroom. But as the foreman read the decision, I could feel a shift of energy, and I noticed that a couple of jurors were glancing at us with kind, sympathetic faces. They had apparently seen through the lies and bluster of the Hyatt lawyers. It was a stunning victory against a mammoth corporation, and it felt both thrilling and surreal. The financial award was primarily based on my father's anticipated income had he lived to retirement age. That was a direct, easy calculation, but then a few hundred thousand dollars was tacked onto this figure for our "pain and suffering." All totaled, the award was $975,000, with 40 percent going to the lawyers and another chunk going to pay back the workman's comp wages that my mother had received from the university. We weren't rich, but we were extremely grateful that my mother wouldn't have to work to pay day-to-day expenses. Equally important was the fact that *Banks v. Hyatt* would now serve as a landmark case for hotel security. The judgment became the precedent for all future hotel liability cases, making it clear that hotels *do* have a duty to protect and warn their patrons from known dangers.

As we flew home to Maine, we all breathed a sigh of relief, believing that we could now, finally, put Dad's death behind us. We were wrong. The Hyatt Regency appealed the verdict all the way to the Louisiana Supreme Court, a process that lasted another five years and kept the wounds open and oozing.

When I left for college in Massachusetts the year after my father was killed, I knew I would never return home to Maine to live—it was too painful. But leaving home was not the escape I longed for. The agony of my father's murder packed up and came right along with me; no matter how fast I ran, it was always nipping at my heels. I soon realized that the two defining facts of my life—that I was from Maine and that my father had been murdered—made finding a peer group nearly impossible, and this left me teetering on the edge of isolation. I missed my friends at home who had lived through the murder with me. They read the newspapers, ate the condolence food, and felt the warm sunlight on their faces as the eulogy echoed through the Newman Center at the funeral. I never had to tell them how bad it was. But when I left home, meeting new people meant figuring out how, when, and where to share this deep, painful, even slightly shameful fact of my life.

The sharing has not gotten easier with time. When I first left home for college, the pain was so raw that settling on a consistent strategy was impossible. I never knew whether sharing my father's murder should be a first-date conversation piece or something better shared down the road, when I was confident that the person would be in my life a good long time. Even today, as a psychiatrist who regularly engages in other people's deepest wounds, I can't discuss it without losing all feeling—the words exit my mouth as though my head were a speakerphone.

At first I was an early teller—I needed to see the person's reaction as a measure of his or her ability to deal with the complexity and pain of my life. In contrast, my sister Nancy was and still is a non-teller, not because it's in the past and irrelevant but because it's so awkward to deal with the inevitable "what's next." What does a person say when he learns that your father was murdered? More than once the statement has been met with watery eyes or stunned silence. Inevitably I read those signals as a sign to take care of the emotional mess I created in the other. It can be a tiring routine.

At some point in these usually brief conversations, justice takes center stage and the obvious question is asked: "Did they catch the killer?" For twenty-five years that question had been the exit strategy that I believed both people wanted. I was able to tidy up the dialogue with a shake of my head and the facts: Two sixteen-year-old boys were arrested, and the shooter was sentenced to life without parole. It was a quick and clean getaway into more normal conversations about work and kids and summer plans. The killer was sentenced to life in prison without parole. End of story. While this tragic event happened to my family, at least justice had been served. The killer was put away and he wouldn't be able to inflict this pain on anyone else. People felt better with that fact, and *I* felt better with that fact.

Back then, the verdict and sentencing—emotionally detached from the reality of a sixteen-year-old boy living in a maximum security prison with adult male killers and rapists—balanced the scary, vulnerable feelings and allowed the relationship to proceed only slightly burdened by the large elephant that had been smashed into a too-small box and tucked away in the relational memory bank. Occasionally I would reopen the box if the relationship deepened or if I'd had a few too many drinks. Alcohol was the only thing that settled the whirling flame in my chest and made the relationship a little safer for the real trauma of that day, that year, that transformative event that has shaped every day of my life since. But those occasions have been rare; mostly, there has been just the wrap-up: "He was sentenced to life in prison without parole." The "he," of course, was only loosely attached to a name, Isaac Knapper, not to a person.

My mother's fear and vulnerability after the murder made her a sitting duck for an abusive man. When I left for college and she and Nancy were suddenly alone in a house that was too big for two, that man came to her door—literally. Ken sold my mother a set of concrete steps for the front entryway, then called for a date. My mother and father were high school sweethearts, and she had no idea what new romance would look and feel like at forty-seven. She politely turned him down the first few times, but he was persistent. I suspect it would have been hard to see my mother with any other man, but when she started seeing Ken regularly, it was devastating. Ken and my father were polar opposites. For starters, he had been divorced three times and was estranged from his adult children. He was also controlling, narrow-minded, and insecure. My mother somehow justified her relationship with him by claiming he was "more like her family." She and my father shared a life of the mind, not the body, and they practiced the typical 1950s division of labor. She was a teacher by training but became a family-focused stay-at-home mom. She and my father would occasionally venture out to a colleague's house, but their time together was largely spent attending our school activities and games. Toward the end of his life they would share an evening walk and often play badminton with our neighbors. But my mother seemed to need more.

She was always more of a free spirit than my father, quick to laugh or dance. She enjoyed life. In one photo taken months after my father died, my mother and Kate are captured dancing in the living room, their bodies slightly blurred by motion, their faces beaming with energy. My father did not dance. When she finally agreed to go out with Ken, she was pleasantly surprised that he liked to do some of the things that she enjoyed. They spent many Saturday nights up the road in Belfast dancing at the Blue Goose. She would even accompany him during the week, driving around the state in his truck, as he sold concrete steps. And he gardened with her, something my father would never do. My mother's green thumb was legendary, and every trip home from college began with the grand garden tour. In mock seriousness she would stroll through the four acres of garden beds, introducing me to each blossom she was holding gently in her hand as though it were a trusted friend. The climactic ending was the rose garden, where she cultivated more than three dozen different varieties, each with its own name. Her favorite, as she loved to say, was "Mr. Lincoln."

The price she paid for Ken's companionship was high. He was insanely jealous of my mother's love for her children, and he often pouted when we came home on breaks from school. Too frequently—and often when he and my mother were home alone with Nancy—he would fly into a fit of rage and storm out of the house, informing her that no one would ever love her the way he does, and that no one would ever put up with her children. Not surprisingly, these exits sent my mother—who had endured the agony of having a husband leave home one day and never return—into an immediate collapse. A way-too-young Nancy was usually left to call one of us for help.

She hid the most abusive moments with Ken from her kids until the last months of her life, when she began to complain openly to me about what a bastard he could be. Near the end of her life, I got a glimpse of his cruelty. One evening, while she was in the hospital with yet another infection, she teetered into the bathroom with her IV pole and collapsed on the floor. When I opened the door and saw her lying there, she looked up at me wide-eyed and said, "Aren't you going to yell at me?" As I gently bent to help her up, she said, "That's what Ken does." I wanted to kill him. Ken remained an excruciating presence in our lives until the day my mother died. And when Nancy was married ten months after her funeral, Ken was a no-show.

Nine years after my dad's death, my mother felt a golf-ball-size lump under her arm. This firm, painless mass immediately awoke memories of her own mother's death from breast cancer just two months before my father's murder. These two events were tightly wired together in her amygdala, the brain's fear center. She was terrified that the mass was cancerous and only superficially reassured by her doctor's belief that it was an inflamed lymph node that she had nothing to worry about. But as the months and then years passed with no resolution of the inflammation, he finally decided to do a biopsy. The results confirmed my mother's worst fear: cancer. And not just any cancer—stage-4 ovarian cancer, which had a five-year survival rate of less than 5 percent.

I had just finished medical school and was in my first year of psychiatry residency when I answered her page. The voice—small, weak, and distant—said simply, "It's cancer." The person attached to that voice was immediately recognizable as the mother collapsed on the couch the night my father died, asking me, "What will we do?" That night there was nothing to do, but that wouldn't be the case this time around. We would all fight to keep her alive.

My mother defied medical predictions by surviving another eight years—six of them with a decent quality of life. But she was never more than a month or two from the next blood test or CT scan, and on her low days she talked of the cancer stalking her like the two teenagers who followed my father down Loyola Avenue before gunning him down. The murder was always lurking somewhere close to consciousness, tugging so many of her life experiences into the trauma of that night. Concrete reminders of the killing stimulated abject terror. When my family learned that Leroy Williams was up for parole after serving seven years of his twenty-one-year sentence, my mother panicked, convinced he would travel to Maine and kill us all.

In the last year of her life, the small seeds of ovarian cancer burst forth, marching through her body like a conquering army. The tumors blocked her colon and ureters and wrapped themselves around her spinal column, stimulating periods of mind-numbing pain. Shortly after Christmas she lay waiting in the hospital for another surgery to remove the spreading tumor mass. The surgical resident assigned to her case entered the room and reported that the head surgeon had suffered a major heart attack. Never a good pre-op sign. Two days later the substitute surgeon soberly declared the surgery a partial success. She had removed as much tumor as she could along with a large chunk of colon, then rerouted my mother's intestines into a colostomy bag that she would wear for the rest of her life. This was an indignity of massive proportions for my mother, a clean freak who bathed two times a day whether she needed to or not. Unfortunately, the tumor around her spinal column could not be removed without leaving her paralyzed from the waist down. As I heard the news, I knew her days were numbered. Ovarian cancer is renowned for its ability to replicate quickly. Leaving the tumor around her spinal cord meant that her pelvic cavity would be filled with cancer within months.

As the cancer advanced, Phil's behavior became more erratic and unreliable. One day, when he was about eight hours late arriving at our mother's house, Nancy and I concluded he must be having an affair. In retrospect, he was likely at a bar fortifying himself for another bedside visit.

My pregnancy with my children, Jayme and Alex, coincided with the last precious year of my mother's life—these two seminal events on a dramatic collision course, and the circle of life painfully personal. Some days it felt as though my body, filling with life, was draining hers. When the conflict of being away from my mother in her last days became too much, I scheduled one last appointment with my ob-gyn. With her okay, I would get my medical records to take to Maine to wait out the birth and death at my mother's home. My babies had other plans—in her office, I was already four centimeters dilated. My partner had left for a short business trip to Santa Fe that morning, and my dear friend Lisa drove me to the hospital rather than to my mother's house in Maine. Eighteen hours later the twins were born via C-section, and that afternoon I called my mom to share the exciting news. She was at home in hospice, exhausted. She had literally stayed alive to meet my two children.

But staying alive was not easy. Months earlier, the pain from the tumor invading her spinal cord had become so debilitating that the doctors installed an external port into the base of her spine. An anesthetic, lidocaine, was pumped into the space to numb the area. While this provided temporary relief from the excruciating pain, the port was the perfect conduit for bacteria to enter her central nervous system, travel up her spinal column, and attack her brain. By the time I called to share the news of the birth she was down to her last few working neurons. Over and over again she asked me how to spell their names and how much they weighed. The information hovered in the space between us and was immediately devoured by the infection ravaging her brilliant mind. When we hung up the phone, the pain and loss were crushing. It seemed clear to me that she might not live to meet my children in person.

But she did live—for twelve more days, long enough to spend a bittersweet afternoon together. My mother was unable to leave her bed, so she lay skeletal and exhausted, drifting in and out of sleep with a child nestled into the crook of each arm. From time to time her piercing blue eyes would gaze at the babies, admiring the ways in which they reminded her of her own newborns. A week later she was in the final stages of dying, with Nancy and Ken by her side. I frantically called Phil, warning him she was hours—not days—from death. She had dodged death so many times in the last year, it was hard to believe that this was the real deal. When he finally arrived and walked into her room, she opened her eyes one last time, smiled weakly and took her last breath.

Phil's drinking increased dramatically after our mother's death in 1998. They had had a special bond, and losing her was the proverbial straw that broke the camel's back. My mother had adored Phil, only half-jokingly calling him "her king." He could do no wrong in her eyes—all faults were easily pushed aside by the memory of his birth at three and a half pounds, with the umbilical cord wrapped around his neck. For her, his difficult arrival in the world explained everything from his explosive temper to the difficulty he had appreciating the impact that his actions had on others. He once borrowed her new Buick, took the car on a wild off-road adventure, and then casually returned it completely covered with mud. No explanation, no apology. And none appeared to be needed—in her mind, the fact that he was born close to death gave him a free pass for life.

I believe our mother's death unleashed my brother's biggest demons. As the years went by, his drinking became intense and predictable. I could track his use by the content of the emails he sent me in the middle of the night. At 1:00 a.m., the first few drinks would have settled his nerves and freed his emotions, allowing him to send sentimental messages about how much he loved me and how no one would ever understand the depth of the bond we shared. I understood this to be shorthand for the traumatic loss and loneliness that he lived with daily, along with a desperate attempt to resurrect the intimacy of our deep childhood friendship. But as the hours went by and the level of alcohol in his system increased, the emails began to darken, from devoted, to despairing, and finally to psychotic, complete with a morbid fixation on the murder. Messages arrived in my email account around four in the morning from "Kiro," an intoxicated CIA agent alter ego who was "on the case" to find and kill our father's real murderer. On more than one occasion, he shared the good news that the assailants had been taken out with a poisonous blow dart to the neck. These episodes left Nancy and me feeling helpless and retraumatized.

Watching my brother's life unravel was like watching a slow-motion train crash. By the time Nancy and I realized that we had to intervene, we knew it was bad, but we had no idea just how bad. Nancy and her husband, Gary, and I arrived at Phil's new apartment, full of dread and unprepared for what we found. The chaos and destruction were disorienting. Papers, dirty dishes, and laundry were strewn about as though an intruder had ransacked the house. Framed photos of our family were smashed, and shards of glass dotted the carpet. Teetering in the middle of all this mayhem was Phil, drunk out of his mind, barely able to stand but still offering a weak half-smile and a slurred hello, apparently oblivious to the squalid conditions in which he was living.

We had a mission that fall day in 2003: to take Phil to his first stint in alcohol rehab. He was in a death spiral, his fragile life collapsing around him. Months earlier, as his drinking escalated, his wife had asked him for a divorce and his boss at a major financial consulting firm in Boston encouraged him to get help. When he refused the offer and denied that he had a problem with alcohol, they let him go. Most devastating was that his drinking was endangering the one indispensable connection in his life—his relationship with his five-year-old daughter, Renee. We had no way of knowing that this would be the first of many unfathomable rock bottoms for our brother. The addiction was devouring him. Living alone with no work to structure his days had fueled a vicious cycle of pain and the need to escape it with alcohol. By the time we arrived at his apartment, he was pretty much drinking vodka and other hard liquor around the clock.

Phil assured us that there was no alcohol left in the apartment, but we had learned not to take his intoxicated assertions at face value. As we searched, Gary's eyes were drawn to a pile of papers scattered across the coffee table. Newspaper clippings of the murder and trial were interspersed with Phil's handwritten notes about Isaac Knapper and Leroy Williams. In a moment that could have passed without notice, Gary made a mental note that Knapper was spelled with a *K* and not an *N*, as he had always assumed.

14

FREEDOM

Isaac Knapper

There was nothing unusual about that spring day in 1989. I was still walking the concrete in Angola and had just finished breakfast when a guard approached me and said, "Knapper, you have a legal visit."

Three things about this announcement caught me off guard. First, I had not retained counsel, so the fact that a lawyer was visiting me was a huge surprise. Second, I was sentenced to life in prison and did not have any legal motions pending that would warrant the need for a lawyer. Third, even if I had the money to retain a lawyer, I would not have done so based on my horrendous legal experience eleven years earlier with Mr. Zibilich.

It took me twenty minutes to go from the dining hall back to my unit to change clothes, be cleared through security, and be seated in the lawyer/inmate visiting area. Within minutes, a young woman of about thirty years old walked into the room. She was beautiful, friendly, energetic, and confident, and given that I had not visited with a woman outside my family for eleven years, her attributes made a special impact on me. Although Laurie White was about to tackle her first case as a defense attorney, she was no rookie. She was a seasoned former prosecutor earning her stripes the hard way, standing toe to toe with Judge Shea, the man who had presided over my conviction in 1979. She was not even a bit nervous.

"It's nice to meet you, Mr. Knapper," she said. "I guess you are wondering why I am here?" She paused for effect. "My name is Laurie White and I am here because I believe you are an innocent man and if you give me the chance, I would like to help you get out of prison." As I heard these words, my mind quickly raced back to Burl Carter.

Burl was a jailhouse lawyer, clever like the famous lawyer Johnny Cochran but without a law degree. He had been sentenced to 198 years in prison for his second armed robbery conviction. Burl and I had shared the same Angola address for the last eleven years, and for some reason he had insisted on working on my legal case. He pushed through my stubbornness, and when I gave him my trial transcript, he read it for a few minutes and said I had a good case. To tell me that after reading the transcript for a few minutes when I had already served eleven years wasn't going to cut it. I just walked away. He couldn't possibly think I believed him. I had no patience. I was the heavyweight champ of Angola and you either came to the king bearing the right gifts or you stayed away. But now, hearing these words from Laurie White, I remembered Burl's exact words just a few days earlier. In a conversation that took place by my bunk, he said, "Isaac, you are innocent and I am going to help you get out of prison."

I could not help but think that there are no coincidences in life. Think about it—after serving eleven years of a life sentence in the worst prison in America, two people who had never met each other told me that I was an innocent man and that they were going to help me get out of prison. The fact that those two statements were made independently, within days of each other, made me think that maybe, just maybe, there might be hope that my innocence could be proven once and for all. But in Angola hope is a dangerous thing. I had seen far too many guys convinced their cases would be overturned, only to have those hopes crushed by a system of retributive justice that is quick to convict and slow to admit that they had convicted the wrong man.

"Mr. Knapper, I promise that if you give me an opportunity, I will fight to win your release." When Laurie spoke these words, I smiled and knew in my heart that somehow, in some special way, things were going to change for me. I was still locked up, but after looking into the eyes of Laurie White and seeing her sincerity and passion, I knew that God had sent me an angel. Her smile was intoxicating, and I felt something I hadn't felt in years and something few in my position would dare to experience: hope.

Ms. White's very first case would not be an easy one. A life sentence for murder in the first degree was not easy to get overturned. But from the start, Laurie was intensely and emotionally involved in my criminal case and my civilian life. Unfortunately, before meeting Laurie White, my experience with defense lawyers was largely shaped by Mr. Zibilich, who was not fit to clean dirt off her shoes. In the first week of visits, she provided details of my case that I had never been made aware of. Her approach was dynamic. If a wall appeared in front of her that she could not scale, she would simply knock it down.

Shortly after I met with Laurie, Burl said he needed to get the police report from my case file. I had never heard of the police report, certainly never heard my original defense lawyers discuss it. Burl explained that every accused criminal would have a report in their file documenting the results of the police investigation. Burl seemed to think that finding it would be key to proving my innocence and getting me released from prison.

I sat down on the bench next to the locker and motioned for Burl to do the same. That's when I told him about Laurie White's visit earlier that day and that I thought it would be best to contact her directly. He seemed excited by this news and offered to write to her that very day.

Thinking out loud, I said, "And I will call the one person in this world who can get their hands on that police report." Burl just waited for me to finish the thought; I rose to my feet, shut my locker, turned to Burl, and said, "Momma—who else?"

When I called Momma a few days later, her voice was filled with excitement as she exclaimed, "I got it, honey! I got it!" I dropped the phone receiver and quickly picked it back up. The police statement, known as the "Dillman report," consisted of a thick file that included everything about my case.

Shortly after reviewing the report, Burl came to find me as I was working out. "Champ, champ, you're going home," Burl hollered as I hit the punching bag.

I stopped boxing and sat down with Burl, and he briefly explained that the Dillman report contained the "smoking gun" that would prove the prosecution had convicted the wrong man. He didn't stop there. He also let me know that I needed to read the entire report, saying there was something in it that was so explosive that he had had to read it three times to believe it. Despite my prodding him for information, Burl left the file with me and walked away. There I sat, in the middle of the Angola boxing gym, sweating from my workout, dirty from a long day, but absolutely intrigued at what might be so significant in the file. I picked it up and began to read.

"Derek Robertson? Can't be," I said to myself. My palms became sweaty and my heart raced so fast I could hear it beating. My mind thought back to the hundreds of days I had spent with D-Monster in Angola and how he had always told me that he "knew I was innocent." At the time I just thought he was being kind, but as I read the Dillman report I learned that D-Monster had had firsthand knowledge of my innocence. The Dillman report contained information that D-Monster had been one of three young Black men arrested for attempted armed robbery just a week after the Banks murder and one block from the Hyatt Regency Hotel. Even more damning was the fact that the gun used in that robbery was the same gun that had killed Dr. Banks. My first inclination was to drop the report and run to wherever D-Monster was and unleash eleven years of anger and frustration on him. Perhaps by God's providence, at that very moment he was locked up in the "hole," and I would never see him again. I set the report down, stared at the ground, and thought back to all D-Monster and I had been through since our incarceration in Angola. There was no one closer to me in the world during my time in Angola and he held the keys to my release—yet he never said a word.

This should have been the happiest day of my life and yet I had never felt more alone. All I could think of at that moment was how badly I wanted to call Momma.

After D-Monster was released from Angola, he came to see me but I wasn't around. His lifestyle would cause him to strike again. He pulled the trigger one night, killing two Cubans over a kilo of drugs and was subsequently caught with the gun and the kilo. While he beat the murder charges, he was sentenced to another fifteen years for the gun and the drugs. When he was released after eight and a half years, he again tried to find me, but to no avail. Finally, he was killed in a drug deal gone bad. D-Monster lived by the gun and died by the gun. So would end another chapter of friendship.

Once I got the report, I called Laurie White and asked to see her as soon as possible. The very next day, Laurie, Burl, and I sat discussing the Dillman report, realizing that it had not been shared with my lawyers in the original trial. Laurie suggested that we file a motion for an evidentiary hearing where a judge would hear this new evidence and determine whether to overturn my conviction. There was one big problem: the judge who would preside over the hearing would be the same Judge Shea who had convicted me. She said not to worry, that if it were denied, she would simply go over his head. Well, sure as rain, it was denied. It was hard for me to believe good things could actually happen, given all that I had lived through and seen over the past eleven years. Burl and Laurie put their brilliant minds together and filed another motion that took ninety days to be heard.

My life was moving along in the right direction with Laurie White at the helm, armed with the Dillman report, but one huge obstacle stood in our way: Judge Shea. He would never allow my case, or any other case he previously ruled on, to be overturned. Laurie knew she had to get my criminal case out of Judge Shea's courtroom. In a brilliant legal maneuver, Laurie arranged for Judge Shea's nephew, a lawyer who also believed I was innocent, to sit in her place as counsel at my next hearing. She knew that Shea could not hold court with a relative as my defense counsel—this would be a conflict of interest. It worked, and Judge Shea moved the case to Judge Winsberg's courtroom for a bond hearing. Based on this new evidence, the bond was set at $250,000. Momma got the money for me and once she did, I was free to go. That evening the guard yelled to me, "Knapper, get your things, you're rolling out."

That night was perfect for a walk out of hell. It was warm and free and I felt so beautiful. I had gone to the penitentiary one month after my seventeenth birthday, and I was released one month after my twenty-ninth birthday. Laurie White was the first to hold me at the breaking of the news. Momma would be the next and there wasn't a dry eye around me. That day my arms couldn't reach around everyone who had showed up. My family, having endured the whole ordeal as well, were all by my side. They never quit believing in me.

Momma never gave up hope. She knew that one day God would shine his light on me. My family watched as a young teenager left to serve his life in prison and now seemed to return a free man. There are no words to describe what it is like to walk out of prison after receiving a life sentence.

But I was not yet a free man. I was free on bond, and in the back of my mind there was still a bit of worry, as I still needed to go before the court for one last hearing. Being around civilized people was not enough to make my mind forget what I had lived through. I had regular flashbacks to my time in prison that left me feeling sick, and while the anger and hostile feelings were gone, deep inside my heart there was a wound that I knew would never heal.

The week for the final court hearing approached quickly. Laurie was at my side and my family behind me when my name was called by Judge Winsberg. Michael Riehlmann stood beside me as Laurie's stand-in when I approached the bench. Judge Winsberg read the papers in front of him and looked at me. No one was breathing. Then he said, "You are free to go." Those were the sweetest words I'd ever heard.

When I turned around to face the exit, my whole family was there to welcome me home for good. I took a couple of steps and then, overcome with emotion, I collapsed to my knees, weeping. Laurie grabbed me, and then Momma hugged me, along with my family. I pressed so many hearts against me on that day. It is one of those days in life I will never forget! My sister Hazel outdid herself in preparing a feast for me with all the fixings, including my favorite chicken and dumplings.

Laurie and her husband, Tom, had a couple of surprises for me. First, they leased a building and set up a complete boxing gym just for me. It was a one-story structure on Conti and Lopez Streets in New Orleans and had everything from the front office to the showers. I would call it Percy's Corner in honor of Percy Pugh. Then Laurie and Tom presented me with their last surprise of the day—a set of keys to a blue 450 SE Mercedes Benz.

The things Laurie and Tom did for me at that stage of my life were, and still are, locked deep in my heart and are a reminder of our deep friendship. I wish that anyone who walks out of prison can walk into the free world with as much support as I had. My life wasn't about getting high or drinking. The support allowed me to pick up where I had left off when my life had been hijacked at the age of sixteen.

15

Shocking News

Amy Banks

When the Louisiana Supreme Court made a judgment in our favor in 1985, the relief was palpable. The nightmare was finally over; we could breathe again. There would always be a line of demarcation in our lives—before and after April 12, 1979—but there finally could be real traction in our attempts to put this hellish event behind us once and for all. So when we discovered in 2004, twenty-five years later, the shocking news that Isaac Knapper had been released from prison in 1992, we felt as though we'd been sucker-punched. This was a body blow that tore open the brittle scar, releasing the agony and confusion of the murder that had been only slightly dulled by the passage of time. As the familiar nightmares and flashbacks returned, it was clear that I was no better equipped to deal with my father's death at age forty-three than I had been as a teenager. And the stakes were even higher now, because I was desperate to protect my six-year-old twins from the trauma of losing a parent, either physically or emotionally.

My brother-in-law Gary is a quirky guy, little-boy cute with sleepy eyes like Robert Kennedy. He is a self-labeled "inveterate people searcher" who spends hours at the computer every day for work and pleasure. He often Googles old high school friends to see how their lives have turned out, curious about whether their high school persona was authentic or simply a facade that eventually fell away when the person tumbled into the real world. A few months after Phil went to rehab for the first time, Gary sat at his desk at work with a little time on his hands. He typed "Isaac Knapper," with a *K*, into a search engine. This wasn't the first time that Gary had searched for Isaac's name, but it was the first time he had done so since that night a couple of months earlier when he had taken Phil to rehab, the same night he had stumbled across the proper spelling of *Knapper* in the wreckage of Phil's apartment.

He was stunned when the first story that popped up detailed Knapper's 1992 release from prison. To this day, he remembers the shock as he sat back in his chair and thought, *Holy shit!*, then tried to figure out how he would break the news that he knew would unleash a firestorm within our family. And that's exactly what happened—the news was crushing, the emotional equivalent of a level-eight earthquake or a tsunami. It was like having a cemetery unearthed, the coffins tipped over and opened, the bodies flung about in various states of decay. It was the day the wrap-up story unraveled, flinging my family back to April 12, 1979, and releasing the bound-up grief, anger, and deep confusion of living in a world that makes no rational sense.

Knapper's release from Angola was only one piece of a remarkable story that had been big news in the city of New Orleans, where his wrongful conviction appeared to be more evidence of prosecutorial injustice from an allegedly corrupt district attorney's office led by Harry Connick Sr. Not only had Isaac Knapper been exonerated for the crime of murdering my father, but after his release from Angola he had become an accomplished amateur boxer who came close to making the United States Olympic team that went to Barcelona in 1992. Newspaper articles from that time reported that a young attorney named Laurie White had uncovered exculpatory evidence that had been withheld from Isaac's defense team during the trial. Most of the stories agreed that had this information been available to the defense team at the time of the trial, there was a good chance that it would have raised reasonable doubt in the minds of the jurors. In fact, the evidence appeared so damning that had the defense been aware of it, the Knapper case may well have been thrown out long before trial.

I am still not sure what was more shocking at the time of the discovery, that he was released from prison and was a celebrated athlete, or that my family was never told. Nothing—complete silence from the DA's office. There was, and still is, no logical explanation as to how this happened. I'm not talking about the dogged pursuit of the truth on the part of his lawyer, Laurie White; or about the long years it took to gain his release after the discovery of the prosecutorial misconduct; or even the fact that a young, poor Black man was wrongfully convicted of murder. Sadly, all of this was par for the course in the U.S. "justice system" in 2004. More shocking, at least to my family, was that not one person in the New Orleans Police Department or the Orleans Parish District Attorney's office could muster the energy or the courage to make a phone call or send a letter to the family of Ronald Banks to inform us that the killing of our father was now an unsolved crime, an open murder case. Perhaps they figured we were comfortably tucked away in Maine and would never find out. Perhaps they didn't want to stir things up and make more work for themselves. Or perhaps we were nothing and nobody to these folks, interchangeable names and faces in a long struggle to stop the rampant violence in New Orleans.

What my family was not—and certainly what Isaac Knapper and his family were not—were real human beings with deep scars from this tragic event. I am sure no one in the DA's office imagined what it would be like for me to have to tell my children that their grandfather had been murdered, or that I would then have to update that story and share with them that a young man, just their age, had been railroaded into a conviction and that no one cared enough about him then, or our family now, to let us know. They couldn't imagine the conversations I would have with my son—who grew up looking more and more like his grandfather—about how this happened. The hard questions he asked about justice, the value of one person's life, and even the possibility that Isaac Knapper did kill my father. Because, certainly, if anyone in the DA's office imagined the ripple effects that this would have on my family and the families of my siblings, they would have done the right thing—they would have called and simply said, "We were wrong." But they didn't, and we lived for twenty-five years under the false notion that justice had been served, that bad things happen but the legal system can help put some closure to it. And now, that deep, old scar had been ripped wide open. And my family didn't know where to go or whom to trust as we again sought some explanation and some justice for our murdered father.

Nancy was thirty-four years old the year her husband uncovered the latest mess in New Orleans. As she grew up, those who knew our father would say she was the most like him physically and mentally. She inherited his height, big feet, and intense curiosity about history. She was completing her doctorate in history at Columbia University, no small coincidence given that my father was headed there for his PhD—at least until my mother became pregnant with Phil and the move from small-town Maine to New York City simply became incompatible with her vision of the life of a competent and successful mother. Nancy's research skills were just what our family needed: to discover the truth behind Isaac's exoneration and the question of prosecutorial misconduct.

Michael Perlstein, a well-known writer at the New Orleans *Times-Picayune,* had documented Isaac's release and his subsequent rise and fall in a series of newspaper articles that, thanks to the miracle of the internet, were easy to track down. From those we discovered some of the key basic facts about Isaac's release from Angola. Apparently, Laurie White—the young lawyer who had once worked closely with Judge Frank Shea, who presided over Isaac's criminal trial in 1979—agreed to look over the case file sometime in 1989. In it she found a report that contained exculpatory evidence that apparently hadn't been presented at trial. The most damning "Brady" material (so named after the 1963 *Brady v. Maryland* ruling, which said that the prosecution team has a legal obligation to turn over all evidence to the defense team prior to a trial) appeared in the police report written by detective John Dillman. Within the file was a memo sent to Dillman from Sargent Italiano alerting him to an armed robbery that was committed just a week after my father's murder. He wrote, "It should also be mentioned that the District Officers' report reflected that the general physical description, along with clothing description of these three subjects closely matched the description of the two wanted subjects in the murder of Ronald Banks." This armed robbery took place only a block away from the Hyatt Regency and a few days later ballistics tests proved that the chrome-plated pistol used in the April 19th robbery was the same gun used to murder my father! It is inconceivable that a defense team would have possessed this information but not used it to defend their client.

Nancy contacted the New Orleans Police Department, who made it clear that the case was entirely in the hands of the District Attorney's Office. However, when Nancy contacted the DA's office asking for clarity about how the conviction was overturned, why it wasn't retried, and why we weren't contacted, they offered very little. Someone from the DA's office researched the case, and the only information he could find was that when the conviction was overturned, the DA's office decided not to pursue the case any further. He told Nancy that because he was unable to locate the internal case file, he could only speculate on the rationale behind the decision. Further calls by Nancy to the DA's office requesting that the case be reopened simply went unanswered.

When it became clear that our family meant little or nothing to the DA's office, Nancy decided to contact Julia Sims, Louisiana's leading victim-rights advocate at the time, to see if we had any recourse. Her response was chilling. Even though the DA's office had a legal obligation to inform the victim's family of an overturned conviction, our story was all too common in Louisiana, and the DA's office apparently couldn't be held responsible for these types of errors and omissions.

After hitting a dead end with government agencies that were either unwilling or unable to help us decipher what had happened in the aftermath of our father's murder, Nancy switched strategies. The new plan was to bring media attention to the injustice and force the DA's office to help us access the legal records. In buckshot fashion she contacted Michael Perlstein at the *Times-Picayune;* the editor of the *Camden Herald*, the local paper in the town in which my parents had grown up; and the news editor at the *Bangor Daily News,* one of the papers that had originally covered our father's murder and Isaac Knapper's conviction. In the letter she wrote to Michael Perlstein, she captured both the distress and the many questions our family had:

"My family is obviously sickened by the whole situation. Both my uncle and my older brother attended Knapper's original trial, and my family did take some comfort in knowing that the person who killed my father was in prison. While it seems clear that there were some severe irregularities in the DA's original case against Knapper, and we feel terrible that an innocent man could have spent almost ten years in prison for a crime he did not commit, we are most upset by the fact that no one in the DA's office ever contacted us to inform us that Knapper had appealed his case, and most important, that his conviction was overturned and he was released from prison. If we had been contacted in 1991, we could have pressured the police department to reopen the case or could have perhaps pursued additional options. As far as I can tell, no one contacted Leroy Williams (who served seven years in prison for his role in the murder), who was with Knapper when he allegedly shot my father, nor did anyone contact John Hakola, the only other living witness to the crime. Moreover, my family has also been upset about the fact that while there have been numerous news stories written about the case, not one journalist ever contacted our family to discuss this matter.

"Ideally, we would like to have the case reopened, but as you mentioned in your email, that does not seem very likely. At the very least, we would like access to the court files and the police reports about the case (which the DA's office claims it no longer has and the court cannot give us because of the expungement order), which could at least provide us with some additional information so we could have some closure on this matter. For example, in one of the stories that you wrote about the case, there was reference to the fact that around Knapper's neighborhood, the conventional wisdom was that someone else was responsible for my father's murder and that Knapper was revered for not revealing that person's identity. While this seems an unlikely scenario, the point is that we feel that our family has a right to be given some clarification about the case."

She wrote to the popular criminal investigation show, *Cold Case Files,* in an effort to generate some interest, and also reached out to attorneys Laurie White and the original prosecutor, David Paddison. To cover all bases, she even wrote to Stephen Murray, the New Orleans lawyer who had represented our family in the civil lawsuit against the Hyatt Regency.

Paddison seemed eager to share his impressions about the case. In his memory, after the conviction had been overturned, the case was remanded to the New Orleans criminal court, where Knapper was supposed to be retried. But in 1993, the assistant district attorney, Raymond Bigelow, chose not to retry Knapper, entering "nolle prosequi" (do not prosecute) into the record. According to Paddison, the DA's office couldn't locate Leroy Williams, the alleged co-assailant and the only person to identify Knapper at the trial.

In his conversation with Nancy, Paddison wondered aloud whether Knapper had anything to do with Leroy Williams's disappearance, although he was quick to point out that he had no proof to support this. Regarding the accusation that the prosecution withheld information about the three men who had held up another couple with my father's murder weapon just a week after his death, Paddison simply said that the men were good friends of Knapper and Williams. Guilt by association taken to the nth degree, it seemed to us. Clearly, in Paddison's mind any one of these bad eggs could have done the shooting, as though it actually didn't matter because they were simply interchangeable.

The more people Nancy contacted, the more confusing the story became; the good guys and the bad guys had almost become indistinguishable from each other. As far as we could tell, Michael Perlstein, the writer from the *Times-Picayune*, offered the most coherent account of the story in a series of three articles he wrote about the Knapper case in 2001. These pieces revealed the following:

Isaac Knapper entered Angola in 1979 at the age of seventeen and used boxing to survive the violent prison environment. In fact, he held the Louisiana State Penitentiary title for nine years.

A jailhouse lawyer (essentially another convict who had developed an interest and expertise in reviewing other inmates' cases) found a police report (the Dillman report) that contained two details not revealed at Isaac's trial. The first was that John Hakola's description at the time of the murder of the clothing worn by the shooter didn't match his testimony at the trial. The second, more critical, fact was that the murder weapon used to kill my father had been confiscated by police a week after my father's murder; it had been found in the possession of three men who had been arrested for an attempted robbery just a block from the Hyatt and who fit the description given by Dr. Hakola of my father's assailants.

Laurie White agreed to review Isaac Knapper's case in 1989 and was shocked to discover in the Dillman Report the exculpatory evidence that had clearly not been shared with the defense team prior to his trial. Based on this new evidence, she filed a new appeal with the Louisiana Supreme Court, which subsequently decided to overturn Isaac's conviction.

When Isaac was released from prison in 1992, Laurie White and her husband, Tom, an investment banker, set up a gym and managed his boxing career. They even hired his old coach, Percy Pugh, as a trainer. The gym represented a number of young amateur boxers in New Orleans. With this support Isaac went to the Olympic boxing trials, where he fought his way through the losers bracket and eventually ended up with a bronze medal, losing in the last fight to a man thirty pounds heavier than he was.

Laurie White pursued a lawsuit against the Orleans Parish District Attorney's Office to get monetary compensation for the years in which Isaac was wrongfully imprisoned. The lawsuit was dismissed but it did eventually lead to the passage of a new law in Louisiana that allows others to sue the DA's office for wrongful conviction.

Laurie White then attempted to bring David Paddison up on an ethics charge for withholding Brady material. An unprecedented disciplinary hearing was held to review the accusations that Paddison purposefully withheld the police report from the defense team. A committee of two judges and a businessman ruled two to one in favor of Paddison.

Throughout this long, tortuous process, Paddison and the DA's office continued to believe that they had arrested the right man all along—that Isaac Knapper had killed my father.

As Isaac's professional boxing career waned and his income became insufficient to support a wife, girlfriend, and children, he began to traffic cocaine. He was eventually arrested by the feds in 1999, and in order to protect his family and friends, pleaded guilty in 2000 and was sentenced in April 2001 to another twenty years in federal prison.

This new information destroyed the neat ending of my wrap-up story. I could no longer say "he was sent to prison for life without parole." In fact, my father's murder case was now unsolved, unopened, and pretty much uninteresting to anyone except my family. The bigger story now was the wrongful conviction of a talented young man.

As 2004 drew to a close, the energy needed for our fight waned. The story had gotten worse, and the internal feelings were even more complicated, but we felt helpless—we had hit an institutional dead end in our efforts to have justice served. A few newspaper articles had been written (in the *Bangor Daily News* and the *Times-Picayune*) and a few people continued to take notice, but most of all, life went on. By early 2005 we were ready to move on as well, even though a layer of confusion and anger had been added to our buried feelings of grief. The case would remain unsolved, and the trauma was now a wide-open, festering wound.

As I struggled to digest this new information, a deep, unsettled place opened up in my chest. To this point, justice had been an abstract idea that helped balance the overwhelming helplessness of losing my father. But justice had just gotten a whole lot more complicated. I had felt moved and sad when I heard my brother's description of the wails of disbelief and grief from Isaac's family when the verdict was read, but I didn't yet know just how unfair the world could be, and I had no inkling that innocent people were routinely swept into a legal system that worked against them rather than for them. Justice was no longer about my father's death and what my family had lost; there were now even bigger issues: A young man's life and dreams may well have been obliterated, seamlessly and without guilt, by a DA's office that simply didn't see him as a valuable human being.

For twenty-five years, Isaac Knapper had lived in my mind as a troubled young man who had learned violence in the projects and had simply acted out what he knew. It was a naïve story line, but it had allowed me to stay distantly sympathetic to him and his family. I felt better about myself for that, but I had no idea that I was participating in the same process that had secured his fate in the first place.

But Isaac had now come to life with far more complexity. Reading the descriptions of him given by friends and family in old newspaper stories made my head spin:

> "I've never seen anyone with so much heart," said Laurie White, the attorney who successfully appealed Knapper's murder conviction. "In Angola, he survived by boxing. He went there as a small, skinny kid and he fought his way through every weight class. When he got out, everybody said he was too old to box amateur, but he tried anyway. And he came so, so close."

Arthur Mitchell, a former Angola inmate, says that fellow inmates cheered Knapper's victory. "About ninety percent of the people who [say they were convicted wrongly], you just ignore it," Mitchell said. "But with Knapper, people always believed him. He had that sincere type of innocence. The crime didn't fit the character."

According to those close to Knapper, he just seemed too childlike and gentle to commit such a cold, thuggish crime. Antonio Johnson, who grew up with Knapper, said, "He was a role model out here and in prison. Didn't drink, didn't smoke, didn't curse. He was a good young man who took care of his mother. He was the kind of guy that, if you told him you liked the jacket he was wearing, he'd take it off his back and give it to you."

When Knapper was released, he was a legend in his old neighborhood.

"When he got back, he was like a celebrity," childhood friend Russell Johnson said. "Between the boxing and the publicity about his case, everybody was pulling for him… he was just a baby when he went to prison, but he was able to hold his own, able to knock people out in the boxing ring."

And there was one other thing, Johnson said—a merit badge that exists only on the streets: "He stayed locked up twelve years and didn't rat anybody out. Word was out about who really did that killing, but he never said anything. That made him a hero when he finally got out. He was like a prisoner of war coming back home."[1]

As I read these descriptions and Isaac began to seep into my bones, a great rift developed inside me that was filled with confusion, anger, sadness, and even guilt. Did I believe the prosecution could have railroaded a young, poor Black man?

As 2004 turned into 2005, Nancy managed to get a couple of newspapers to write articles about the case, but the legal system continued to offer no help whatsoever. Then the shit hit

---

[1] Micheal Perlstein. *Times-Picayune*, April 14, 2001.

the fan again. When it seemed as though things simply couldn't get any worse, they did. In April 2005, after discovering that I had the same genetic loading for ovarian and breast cancer that had ended my mother's life, I was diagnosed with ovarian cancer. Pursuing justice for our father's murder would have to take a back seat to surgery, chemotherapy, and the immediate fight for survival. Meanwhile, just four months later, New Orleans was devastated by Hurricane Katrina, and Nancy and I assumed that like so much of the rest of the city, any actual records of the murder or trial had been destroyed.

16

Fighting Again

Isaac Knapper

My life was hijacked when I was arrested for the Banks murder at sixteen. At the time, my future was brighter than most young men growing up in the projects. I had been training for the Junior Olympics and boxing offered me a realistic path out of poverty. Those precious thirteen years I spent in Angola not only stole my prime years as a boxer but also shaped my development from a teenager to a grown man. While friends and siblings were dating, working, going to school, and even building their own families, I was locked in a small cell fighting for my life every single day. The energy of my prime years was spent fending off rapists and murderers in prison. The deprivation and trauma of those years fueled an intense work ethic and focus at the gym and an equally intense longing for and fascination with women after I finally shed my boxing gloves.

When I was finally released, I wasn't sure what to expect from other people. I knew that close friends and family had believed in my innocence all along and supported my family through the years, but what about people I had yet to meet? The response was incredible; I was treated like a war hero instead of a man who had just gotten out of prison for a crime he hadn't committed. Not in my wildest imagination could I have anticipated that people would actually show me sympathy and compassion for the injustice of being falsely convicted. The sleazy tactics the detectives and prosecutors used to convince the jury I was guilty of murder surprised few. It seemed everyone had a brother, uncle, or friend who had been picked up on questionable charges. It was a shock to walk out of prison after thirteen years, but a miracle to step into a dream world where so many people extended a helping hand. Everywhere I went I was treated like a champion on a grand tour of the planet.

Fourteen years after my arrest I started preparing for the actual Olympics, training daily in Percy's Corner. My quest to make the U.S. Olympic Boxing Team for the 1992 Barcelona Games started on a high note when I won the Los Angeles Golden Gloves. Three nights, three fights, three wins. From there we traveled to the Gulf State Tournament: two nights, two fights, and two more wins.

Then I faced elimination bouts in Bay St. Louis, Mississippi. My first fight was a win, and probably the most unusual match of the night. While chasing my opponent in the second round, I threw a hard right hand at him and knocked out the referee. The punch was so hard that the referee rolled over three times.

Most men I hit would simply fall, but the guy I was fighting in Bay St. Louis was different. I wish I had hit him rather than the referee with that right hand. I did eventually catch the fighter with a combo, however, and his corner tossed in the towel. Two more nights, two fights, and two wins.

The next and final stop was Marquette, Michigan, where I fought in the cruiserweight class. If I won there, I was headed for the Olympic trials and a shot at going to Barcelona. The radio stations in New Orleans had been following my progress—I won my first four fights by decision—and now the stage was set for the finals. This would be, by far, the biggest step in my boxing career.

My opponent was from Maryland and his trainer from the school of boxing knowledge. They knew I was coming and unstoppable if he fought me directly. Their strategy to punch and run was the perfect antidote for my aggressive style. His managers told him to stay away from me and he followed their instructions perfectly. He was both a clever puncher and a great runner, and I couldn't land my heavy shots as he effectively dodged to survive my power. My hat was off to him when the decision was returned in his favor.

Everyone thought I had won, and that would have been tremendous. But I didn't feel as bad as everyone else did, because I had given my best during those five days—everything I had went into every punch. The *Times-Picayune* would report years later what is now an obscure footnote in boxing history: "Knapper came within one fight of representing the U.S. in Spain. As a 192-pound heavyweight, fresh from the prison circuit, Knapper fought his way through the loser's bracket of the Olympic trials, stunning more than a dozen opponents until he was finally beaten by a fighter with a thirty-pound weight advantage. Had he won, he would have had a shot at unseating the eventual U.S. Champ." Instead, my amateur boxing career was over.

Just six weeks after the Olympic trials, my professional career began with a win against William Knorr on August 18, 1992, in Pensacola, Florida. Early in the fight my opponent was fading against the ropes, and I doubted he would last the round. He hadn't recovered from the third-round pounding I had given him, and when I knocked him down with a right cross, I was sure by the way he fell that he wasn't getting back up. Much to my surprise he stood up at the seven count and was saved by the bell. Still, I managed to score a convincing win.

After the fights that night I met with the professional boxer Roy Jones, who said he hadn't seen many cruiserweights with my speed and power and invited me to join his camp. My second professional fight took place in September 1992 against Willie Washington of Metairie, Louisiana. Willie was also new to the professional boxing circuit, and he wasn't ready for my hard style of punching. The match stands out for two reasons. First, it was the shortest fight of my career—I knocked him out cold just a minute and thirty-eight seconds into the first round. Second, Willie's family had a ringside seat next to mine, and each side was trying to out-yell the other. The early finish didn't go over well with Willie's family, and when I turned to wave to my family, I noticed a crowd of police security between the two groups, who were outside the ring fighting. Fortunately, no one was hurt but Willie.

My first real setback in boxing was a broken hand I suffered while sparring. I never told my manager, Percy, about it and in fact, I beat Don Johnson by TKO in the third round of my next fight with the broken hand. At the end of my first professional year of boxing I was 3-0 and Tom and Laurie began to look for tougher fights for me. They had high expectations for me and we all had one goal in mind—winning a championship. After taking eight weeks off to heal my hand, I started my second year as a pro with my first loss to a counterpuncher named Ken Jackson. Though I may have been rusty from my time away, I have no excuse for that fight. He was the better boxer that night.

While I was totally committed to becoming a champion boxer, I know now that I was also distracted. I had been in prison from age sixteen to twenty-nine, and when I came out, Cupid was stalking me at every turn. After my release, it was very hard for me to control my attraction to women. I had known puppy love before heading off to prison, but never a woman's love. It was irresistible, and I couldn't turn around without a woman smiling at me. After the years of violence in Angola, I literally craved the softness and comfort of being with a woman.

Sequin, a beautiful woman I'd known when I was fourteen and who had sent letters to me in Angola, had never given up her dream of being in a relationship with me. We would meet up occasionally after I was released, and she eventually gave birth to my first child, a daughter named Sasha, who is now a beautiful young woman. Cupid's arrow hit me again, and I fell in love with Mary Campbell—although I called her "Nickie"— the moment I laid eyes on her.

While I was still in prison, my mother had a restaurant where Nickie worked part-time while going to college. She first saw me in a boxing photo that Momma had hung behind the counter. Nickie asked her if she could write me a letter, and we started to correspond. Not long after my release, Nickie and I began to date, and in July 1993, Isaac III was born. My first two children, Isaac and Sasha, were born five months apart, attended the same school, and became great friends—without knowing that they were actually brother and sister (their teacher once remarked that they looked like twins). Nickie was unaware that Sasha and Isaac were siblings until the kids were seven years old. In Angola, there was no opportunity to develop the skills needed to build an integrated life and my personal life was getting more and more fragmented and complicated.

At one point I was scheduled to fight in Canada and had to go to Roach Medical Labs for a blood test in order to travel internationally. There I met a lab technician, Denise Clayton. We had been classmates fifteen years earlier, and she had grown up to be a gorgeous woman. The moment I walked into the lab I was captivated by her. She looked and felt real, but she appeared almost too beautiful, lovely, and sexually magnetized to be a human female. She would soon become the mother of my third child, Ivory, and they would become yet another part of my increasingly complicated life.

Undoubtedly, by now I had been labeled a dog, but in my defense, it was hard to say no to any of these lovely ladies. I didn't go out into the world trying to hook up with every woman I saw. All three women came into my life in the beginning or middle stage of my professional boxing career, and it became difficult to balance my life as a father with my boxing commitments. Training remained my first priority, and the women in my life understood that, but in my effort to make up for lost time, my focus and energy were inevitably divided.

As my second year of professional boxing got underway in 1993, I stepped up my training routine. I was regularly traveling to other cities to train and to box in sparring sessions with a list of who's-who in boxing. Sessions with Riddick Bowe and John Wesley Meekins from Philadelphia helped me increase my speed. My toughest sessions were with Matthew Saad Muhammad, a four-time world champion. Every time the two of us would spar, it was like a real fight as we went toe-to-toe. I even picked up a heavyweight sparring partner from Angola, Marshall Tillman. At one point I was scheduled to spar with

Evander Holyfield in preparation for his upcoming bout with Mike Tyson. I was chosen because his trainers were looking for someone who threw a punch like Tyson, but unfortunately that fight never happened because of Tyson's legal problems. Nevertheless, working with these pros brought out the best in me, in no small part because I was regularly being challenged to match their speed and punching power.

The next fight, scheduled in Canada, was the worst thing that ever happened to me as a boxer. For starters, Laurie was tied up with a murder trial and Tom was overseas on business, so neither of them could go. Percy, meanwhile, was stuck in the United States—the computer had kicked back his passport application because he was scheduled for a bond hearing on a minor traffic violation. I went ahead without him, assuming that he'd join me later in the week, but he never made it—and working without Percy there was like losing my right arm.

A gym was recommended to me, and I was told it would be easy to find a trainer there who could help me through the fight. The members of the boxing community in Canada were friendly but worried about my speed and power. At the time, it didn't register that all of these guys allegedly helping me were, in fact, in my opponent's corner. Another painful life lesson.

At the weigh-in on the night of the fight, my opponent tipped the scales at 205 pounds. When I stepped on the scales, I knew I weighed around 190, but I suddenly felt something behind me—someone had put a foot on the back of the scales, and my weight mysteriously jumped to 200. Suddenly everyone was talking in French, and I realized what had happened. My appointed trainer assured me that everything was fine, that he had squared it all with the weight official. For my part, I was used to fighting heavyweights in prison, so I wasn't particularly worried, even with the questionable tactics I was witnessing. Off we went into the ring.

While I stayed loose shadowboxing, the trainer applied grease to my face. Everything seemed okay until he wiped grease over both of my eyes. It didn't bother me at first, and he wiped most of it away, even apologizing for getting it in my eyes. However, this "mistake" seemed intentional to me, and sure enough, my eyes were on fire within minutes. I couldn't see a thing. When the bell rang, I moved across the ring, but I still couldn't see. The guy hit me with a heavy right and down I went for the first time in my career. I was up on the two count but was getting tagged from all angles. At the end of the first round the trainer asked me if I was okay, and when I told him that my eyes were on fire and I couldn't see, he stopped the fight. It turns out that someone had put Icy Hot in my grease, and even after being treated by the doctor, it took two days for my vision to return to normal.

In retrospect, I realize that I had set myself up. I naïvely trusted the goodwill of the opposing boxer and his team. I was fair game, especially in a foreign country. I managed to return to New Orleans in one piece, and when I shared the story with Tom, he went off the deep end. He called the trainers in Canada and tore into their asses, but I knew that on the other end of the phone they were probably just laughing. It was spilled milk, nothing to cry over, and it wasn't the worst thing that had ever happened to me. It became another valuable lesson learned about trust.

The next fight was scheduled for Johannesburg, South Africa, and I wanted to make the trip as much as I wanted to fight. Seeing Africa, where my ancestors were from, had a special attraction for me, and Nelson Mandela was scheduled to attend the fight, which was obviously a very special bonus. I continued to train hard, but the incident in Canada lingered in the back of my mind haunting me. This time, thankfully, Percy, Tom, and maybe even Laurie would accompany me to South Africa. I knew I'd have to score a knockout if I wanted to avoid a "hometown decision" in favor of my opponent.

Then, in an instant, the whole picture had changed. Tom called to explain that my scheduled opponent was suffering from food poisoning, and both the fight and the trip were canceled. I was crushed to miss the opportunity of a lifetime.

Shortly after the cancellation of the South Africa trip, I was seemingly struck by a delayed adolescent rebellion. I wanted to stop my two-fight slump, but I wasn't doing the work. I quit running and missed several workouts. I had spent so much time in prison creating a different reality in my mind simply to survive psychically. I began to play mind games convincing myself that I was beyond setbacks. However, the new "adventure" that I had started with Denise Clayton, the lady I'd met while taking the blood test before I went to Canada, was all the excuse I needed to derail me into taking another break from training. Percy would call me every day and get on my case. He was right, of course, but I had fallen in love with Denise and I could not get enough of her. When Nickie and I broke up, I asked Denise to marry me. Then, after being engaged to Denise for a year, we also broke up, and I returned to Nickie to build a life with her and my son, Isaac. Nickie and I married in 1995, but it was tough to forget Denise, so I started seeing her again, even though I was married to Nickie. I was now being pulled in two directions, which left even less room for boxing. Not surprisingly, serious fights emerged on both sides of this drama. When I was with one woman, I felt guilty about the other, and I ended up duplicating everything in an attempt to keep both of them happy. The web I had created was destroying me.

Momma counseled me to choose either Denise or Nickie; otherwise I wasn't being fair to either of them, but I already knew that. I told myself to get it together, to make a decision one way or another, but I couldn't, and I never would. I was in love with two women who were so similar in their likes and dislikes that it scared me. There were times I literally had to stop and think who I was with, and this is how my life began to fall apart a second time. I was living a false reality and pretending to be on top of the world. I should have been chasing my dreams, not women.

Eventually, Percy lured me back into the gym and on to an intense workout program for my next fight, but my heart wasn't in it. I was going through the motions and pretty much just looking for the magic that would pull me back together again. But my experience was not grounded in reality—it was magical thinking. The fight against my next opponent, Clifford Davis, was held in Morgan City, Louisiana, and it should have been easy. All I really had to do was show up. But my intensity wasn't there, and I lost—in my own backyard, no less. I still had the physical ability to fight, but I had lost the most important thing: my heart.

The window of time was closing in on me now—I was a thirty-two-year-old man trying to fight young, fast kids in their twenties. Prison had robbed me of my youth, and those were years I would never get back. Money was becoming a bigger and bigger issue. I wasn't getting paid much for these professional fights, although only a few people knew that. My release from prison and path into boxing had garnered much publicity, so most people assumed I was the "big show" and loaded. My lifestyle was emotionally and financially demanding, and I couldn't answer the bell. I was barely getting by, even though most people who saw me would probably never have sensed that. I tried to present myself as the picture of style, projecting an image of power and money, but the truth was that I was nearly broke. I could feel myself sinking, and it all needed to change very soon. My hope was that Tom would book some bigger-name fights with larger purses attached.

Percy finally managed to provide the verbal glue that would pull me back into the ring. He told me that the three guys I had lost to shouldn't have beaten me in a hundred years. He told me that my training was off and that I wasn't paying attention—I had to get my mind off my women. My next fight was a step in the right direction. I felt good weighing in at 190 pounds. The fight went the full six rounds, with each round dead even until the last. James Hayes won by two points, but I didn't feel bad because after my previous lackluster performances, I had once again given it all I had.

Six months later, Tom signed me to fight a black-tie affair in

Dallas. Joe Wiggins was my opponent, and the fight brought out all the top athletes in Dallas, along with numerous show-business personalities. Wiggins was less than great, and the fight was stopped in the fourth round. I won by TKO.

Tom continued to do his best to line up better fighters and better purses—the latter would let me keep fighting and paying my bills. But my double life was catching up to me, and I couldn't afford to support two families. If I won and went out to celebrate, I worried about spending too much and not being able to cover my bills. Before long I once again found myself being less than diligent about training—hoping that a miracle fight would come along with a big paycheck attached to it.

My mother could always tell when her sun wasn't shining, and she sat down with me to talk about my boxing future. She told me that I was letting my dream of a championship slip away, and that she wanted that as much as I did. I remember telling her, "Momma, I'll do whatever it takes to get my life back on track," but I knew I was lying to my greatest fan.

There would be one more fight. We would step up the quality of fighters and go on national TV to fight Don Mack, a cruiserweight with an 18-1 record. My training routine grew in intensity, and Percy searched for sparring partners that fit Mack's style of fighting.

One day while I was shadowboxing, I heard the door open, and for a split second I thought I saw Scotty Foreman come into the gym. I had to look twice—this guy looked so much like Scotty that it was uncanny. Suddenly, my stomach was full of that raging wind you get when you remember things that were traumatic to you. My mind and body were flooded by images of Scotty back when we first opened the gym after my release from Angola. He had become one of my closest friends, someone who believed in me. When I entered prison, I was just a kid he brought along. When I returned I was a well-seasoned fighter. He kept in touch with me during the dark years in Angola, and when I came out, he wouldn't miss a fight or sparring session on any day of the week.

By the time the new gym was settled Scotty had retired from professional boxing with a 12-8-11 record that was better than it sounded. No doubt remembering the early days when I was a kid and he was the Golden Gloves champ, he wanted to spar with me. As a kid, I couldn't even hit him, but thirteen years later much had changed. He pushed the issue every day, and I would just smile. Like most boxers, Scotty thought he still had it even after years of retirement, and he would hold on to that idea until he stepped into the ring with a younger and stronger boxer who threw the hard reality punch that hit him in the face and brought him back down to earth.

So Scotty persisted, even after I teased him, saying he was way too light for me and that he couldn't be serious. He left the gym one day, and when he returned, he was dressed out in his boxing gear and he began to shadowbox. He still had speed and flash, but when he got into the ring with me this time, our roles were completely reversed. Now he looked like a lightweight, and my speed was faster than he could have imagined. My jabs were thrown with pinpoint accuracy, and I knew I could knock him out whenever I was ready. He knew he had made a mistake after the first few punches.

But he was still the idol that I had respected all those years ago, so I just held back and outboxed him; in my mind, I really just wanted to show him what I had become. I wanted him to be proud of me. And when we finished, he had a new respect for my boxing skills (although it wasn't long before he was telling me, "I'll get back in shape, and then we'll see what can happen"). I knew he wouldn't be back to train, but that was okay, because I knew he would be there with me as I worked through my own training for the Olympics. We even planned to have him in my corner with Kevin Rooney and Tom Wilson—he would stand beside Percy again. This was the dream team that would help me win the gold medal.

Unfortunately, experience has shown me that dreams have a way of shattering, and this would be no different. Scotty was late to the gym one day, and no one had heard from him. Someone finally decided to go to his house and check, and that's where they found him—dead. He'd been shot in the mouth, and no one was talking. In fact, to this day the murder has never been solved. But just like that, another great human being was gone. Scotty lives on in my heart, along with so many other friends who've been killed on the streets of New Orleans. I guess that's why my heart is so heavy.

For the next two months I stayed extremely busy with new sparring partners and heavy bag work. There were periods when I actually felt weak, but I would just ignore the warning signs and attribute them to the fact that the women in my life were wearing me down. So as the date grew closer, I swore off the women and began to feel different than I had before. I was full of energy.

Dan Mack was definitely a step up in the quality of my opponents, but I thought I was ready. The fight was scheduled for a Tuesday night on ESPN, and I wanted to be at my best. I wanted the world to see what I could do. I had trained hard—Percy would wake me every other morning to run eight miles before sunrise—but my appetite was off and I had stopped taking my vitamins somewhere along the line.

We didn't have far to travel—the match was at the Grand Casino in Biloxi, Mississippi. Larry Holmes was fighting Bigfoot Martin in the main event. As I was warming up, Percy asked me what was wrong, but I told him I was fine and that everything was okay. "Well, come on then," he said. "Work!"

I began to worry—something that I had rarely done—and when I entered the ring I felt a little lightheaded. Round one was a feel-out round, and I began to feel better in round two, although my power didn't seem right. Round three was even on the cards, round four was his, and at the bell we both kept punching. The referee stepped in and broke us apart, but as I turned to go back to my corner, Mack reached over the ref and sucker punched me in the back of the head.

This hard right left me dizzy, and if that wasn't bad enough, my girlfriend, Denise, tried to jump into the ring—she was screaming at Mack about his late hit. She kept fighting with my nephew Brian until the security guards finally got her under control. Mack won the split decision—it was his hometown, and that's usually the way those things go.

Tom and Laurie tried to file a protest, saying that Mack should have been disqualified for the punch to the back of my head. I went to the doctor that night, and after his exam I asked him what was wrong with me. He said that the fatigue I'd been feeling could be attributed to a low blood count, adding that it was probably the result of overtraining. I was sure that if I had been at 100 percent, I would have beaten Mack, especially given that at 50 percent of my strength I had managed a split decision. But when I asked him for a rematch, he refused.

I would leave boxing like so many other fighters do when there just isn't enough money to make all of the work that goes into preparing for a fight worth it. Gone was the gym, the roadwork, the long hours of training, the travel, and, most importantly, the glory of knowing that you were the better fighter that night. My career could have gone on, but the fights became insignificant, and they weren't helping me climb the ladder. It was very hard to deal with the fact that it was over. No one could feel it for me, and it was agonizing to know that the best years of my boxing career had been spent in Angola and that I would never get those years back. I was left with the feeling best expressed in the infamous boxing line, "I could have been a contender!" with the crucial addendum, "had I not been wrongly convicted of murder."

17

A Devastating Decision

Isaac Knapper

The cool shower neutralized the heat from my body. I was still sharp and hadn't lost anything, but I just felt that something was missing. While I still dreamed of getting the call for a big fight that would change my boxing destiny, on some level I knew it wasn't coming. Mentally, I had retired from boxing though I never admitted it to anyone and even kept up appearances by training in the gym daily. I was still working for Laurie White but began to feel I had worn out my welcome, that it was not a real job. And I was nearly broke and could barely pay my bills. Meanwhile, people around me were driving big cars, living in big houses, wearing expensive jewelry. No one talked about how they had the money to buy these things.

One Sunday I was in the gym shadowboxing against my worries when a young guy walked over and stood watching me. At the end of my round he approached me, asking how I was doing and commenting on my speed. I just nodded, wishing he would go away. He asked if I was a pro and introduced himself as Lenny. Apparently he had heard that if he wanted to know anything about training he should come to me. He seemed okay, so we talked for a while and I shared a few pointers. We spent the rest of the workout talking about everything and nothing.

Lenny shared that he came from a prominent New Orleans family, that his father was a lawyer, and that he always wanted to learn how to box. After that meeting, we became good friends. Lenny changed his cars almost as often as I changed my socks. The first time I met him he was driving a Mercedes convertible. But other days he drove a Corvette, a Porsche, a van and even a Kawasaki 1000. He seemed to have an endless supply of cars and I assumed they were borrowed from his family. Come to find out, it wasn't that way at all. Lenny owned all of those expensive cars.

Although Lenny tried to hide his drug use, I could tell that on some occasions he was high. I was living a clean lifestyle, hoping against hope that I would get a call for the "Big Fight," which would pay enough to cover my divided life and make up for the many years in prison. At lunch one day, Lenny began talking about how he made his money. The dollar figures were staggering. When I did the math, I realized that his weekly take was more than I had made in all of my pro fights put together.

The first time he asked me to work for him, I refused. A nagging feeling kept telling me that this type of thing would put me right back in prison. But I understood that he was only trying to help me. He could have anything he wanted any time he wanted it, and I—with a wife, girlfriend, and three children to support—needed the money. I grew restless watching him. One day we were together talking about his new Lexus. I commented that it was beautiful but who could afford it. Immediately, Lenny said I could, that he would help, and that I would not need any upfront money. I was curious. He proposed fronting me a package of heroin worth about $150,000. Once I sold it, I would give him $100,000 and I would keep $50,000. While I didn't know anyone I could sell the drugs to, I knew people in the neighborhood who would sell it for me. I took him up on the offer.

As we shook hands on the deal, Lenny smiled and commented, "I can't make it any easier than that."

Yeah, it couldn't get any easier. Instant money, I thought. I wasn't unaware of the drug business—I had grown up in the projects where coke and heroin were everywhere and it was all around me in New Orleans. I had always stayed clear of that life because I wanted to box. However, the drug selling I grew up with was on a small scale; Lenny's organization was different. I entered directly into the top level, where profits were staggering. It didn't take long for the money to start flowing so fast that

I couldn't keep up with it. Suddenly, I had shoeboxes full of bills that blocked out the potential consequences of my actions.

I had been poor my whole life. I went to Angola at sixteen, and when I came out I discovered that the people who had put me in prison were above the law. Realizing that Father Time had the upper hand on me, I began placing more and more of my faith and hope for the future on the civil lawsuit that Laurie White had filed on my behalf against the State of Louisiana for unlawful imprisonment. I remember how people would tell me that my case was literally worth millions because I had endured so many years in Angola prison—the most violent prison in America—for a crime I had not committed. The more people told me what a "slam-dunk" my case was, the more reliant and dependent I became on this potentially huge settlement to provide for my family and my loved ones. I was convinced that for me, justice would finally tip in my favor. However, the huge settlement never came. In fact, the worst day of my life was not when Judge Shea sentenced me to life in prison, but rather that horrible day in 1995 when Laurie White informed me that my case against the State of Louisiana for unlawful imprisonment had been thrown out because, at the time, no law existed that permitted those wrongfully imprisoned to obtain monetary recovery from the State of Louisiana. In fact, in one of those twists of fate usually reserved for Hollywood movies, it was my case that prompted the legislature for the State of Louisiana to change the law so going forward, those who were unlawfully or wrongly imprisoned would be able to pursue monetary compensation for their ruined lives. In a matter of hours, I went from being a man who was only days or perhaps weeks from receiving millions of dollars to someone who now faced the reality of providing for a growing family with what felt like both hands tied behind my back. It was at this point in my life that I made the decision that if certain laws could be used against me, then ignoring certain laws in a way that could benefit me was justified.

This all sounds like a sad song and I admit that I took the

easy way out, but I convinced myself there was simply no other way and I had two families that were now depending on me for support. When Lenny visited me that day while I was training, he had run into an angry, disillusioned Isaac Knapper. I was convinced that the State of Louisiana "owed" me something, and I would collect on this debt.

This is when boxing finally slipped away. There was not going to be that call for a championship fight, there wasn't going to be another fight, period. We simply closed the gym and I walked away and never looked back. My boxing dream came to a silent end. I needed to transfer the same focus and energy I had for boxing toward my new career dealing drugs.

Secrecy was very important, and I kept everything to myself. No one questioned me—friends and acquaintances assumed I earned the money from boxing, and I did nothing to change their way of thinking. Life became so much easier. Lenny's friendship made it simple. If I needed anything, he would see to it that I got it. I could make as much money as I wanted, whenever I wanted. I was in control of my life, or so I thought. Lenny even introduced me to his family, and I became good friends with his sister, Lenjan. It seemed like nothing could go wrong; but how wrong I was.

Late one night, before Lenny's birthday, he called and asked me to come by to see him. I was on my way to Texas for an exchange but said I would come by as soon as I got back. Strangely, Lenny persisted, asking when I would be back. I sensed something was wrong, but I didn't turn around. Instead, I laughed, saying that I was sure he would still be partying when I got back and he should save some for me. He finally backed down and ended the conversation saying, "I love you, Knapper. See ya."

I continued on to Texas, and while I was still driving Lenny took his life by inhaling pure heroin from a huge pile on a table in front of him. He was found dead still sitting in the chair. It's indescribable how bad I felt. He had given me a new life, and I had been the key to keeping him alive that night. And I did not turn around. His funeral felt unreal and I was wracked with guilt. Despite having seen so much death already in my life, this loss affected me greatly.

At the funeral I met many of Lenny's family and friends, and they offered to keep the drugs flowing, but I didn't want it anymore. The last couple of years had been profitable, and I had saved wisely. When I left the funeral, I left the business behind me and swore I would never look back. I had a good home and a nice car, and I had just purchased a liquor store on Galvers Street, a very good source of income. I went to work every day and should have been happy—but the thought of easy money kept pulling on my mind.

After Lenny had been dead for a year or so, I found a business card he had given me in case of a problem. It was easy to convince myself there was a problem, and so I made a call and spoke to Ronnie—and just like that I was back in the business. I switched from selling heroin to cocaine, but the huge influx of cash was the same.

Ronnie was wealthy beyond my wildest dreams, and I was attracted to his success. I learned a couple of things from my business with Ronnie. One was that the more money you made, the more things you could buy. The expenses kept you on the treadmill, ordering more and more weight just to keep up with the bills that had to be paid. I also realized that selling drugs was just as addictive as using drugs. When the user needs a fix, that monkey starts riding his back. When a dealer needs that money, that same monkey starts riding his back.

Just after our first year in business together, tragedy struck again. Apparently someone wanted Ronnie's Lexus more than he did and was willing to kill for it. I was on my way to visit Ronnie in Texas when he was murdered, but I did not find out because I had been pulled over by a Texas State Trooper who searched my car and seized $190,000.00. On paper they claimed they had found $125,000. Someone pocketed $65,000, but it didn't matter; I had lost my money and would have to wait a few weeks to make my next move. I suspected that the combination of my Louisiana plates, expensive car, and being Black aroused suspicion. I hoped the New Orleans newspapers hadn't printed the story because I didn't want Laurie to read it, knowing how disappointed she would be with me. She was cleverer than I gave her credit for; she remained silent and never let on that she knew.

The seizure of a large amount of cash brought the Feds into the picture, and though I was unaware, they began an undercover investigation after that first stop. They used phone taps, surveillance, and high-tech gadgets to catch people like me. About three weeks later I was stopped again; this time they seized $59,000 in cash.

I was still unaware that Ronnie was dead and a couple of weeks later my beeper went off and the number was from Texas. I assumed it was Ronnie, but when I answered, the man on the other end had a Spanish accent. He was Colombian and called me "Jerry." He introduced himself as John, saying he was a friend of Ronnie's and that Ronnie was in the hospital having been shot. He claimed that Ronnie had told him about a man in New Orleans who owed him money. He was trying to collect. But I cut him off, not liking where the conversation was going.

I immediately called Ronnie's mother to see how he was doing and heard the deep sadness as soon as she began to speak. "Ronnie is dead," she said slowly. "He's been dead over two weeks now."

I called John back, angry, asking him what kind of game he was playing, telling me that Ronnie was in the hospital. He told me that Ronnie worked for him and that a man in New Orleans owed him a large amount of money. He wanted my help in collecting it.

He mentioned that Ronnie had always spoken very highly of me. I ended up doing him the favor and got in touch with the man who owed him money. I was also putting two and two together and realized that the guys from Texas could be responsible for Ronnie's death. John was grateful to me when the man squared the debt away and offered his services if I ever needed anything. About a month later business began to go extremely well for me as an opportunity arose for me to deal directly with the Colombian Cartel. In the drug business, any time you can remove a "layer of people" or a "middle man" between you and the end product, your profits increase significantly. I was now living in a two-story house in Tall Timbers, along with the city's civic leaders, high-ranking police commanders, lawyers, doctors, politicians, and corporate CEOs. My closet looked like something from the rich and famous, with customized leathers, shirts, shoes, and suits. I routinely wore diamond watches, rings, necklaces, and belt buckles. Nickie and I needed two large walk-in closets for all the clothing and accessories and, of course, everything I bought my wife, I had to buy for Denise. I honestly didn't care as much about the money as I did about the people in my life. Much of the money was spent keeping family and friends happy.

Nickie regularly stopped me to pat down my pockets before I left the house. She knew I often carried around twenty to thirty thousand dollars and worried I was leaving with too much money. She also knew that if I left with five grand, it would be gone in less than a couple of hours because I take after my mother and can't say no. Whenever family and friends asked me for money, I would give it to them.

One day Nickie and I were riding down Clairborne when I stopped at a red light. A homeless lady walked up to my Mercedes with her hand out. Over my wife's protest, I gave her five hundred dollars, and seeing her reaction was well worth it. First there was confusion as she looked at the money, then at me and then back at the money again. This went on for a few moments. Then, after checking to make sure I knew how much I had given her, came the excitement. She spread the bills out to inspect them and literally jumped for joy, repeatedly saying, "God bless you!"

As we drove away Nickie lectured me about giving so much money away. I responded by saying, "I know, honey. But every time I give from my heart, I am blessed with more. Besides, didn't you see how happy she got?"

Nickie just shook her head again and smiled. "Yeah," she admitted. "She was pretty happy."

I had all the good and all the bad that money could buy. While I was dealing dope, I had kilos of cocaine available to me any time I wanted it. During the next two years, the Colombians and I became good friends; if I needed anything, I would just ask. I was attempting to walk a tightrope, spending way too much money on everything and trying to keep a low profile at the same time. It didn't add up. I wanted to live well, and I wasn't anyone's boss except at my liquor store.

During this time, I kept ignoring the nagging feeling that someone was watching me. In fact, I would later learn that this entire time I was under full investigation by the Feds. Finally, I realized I needed to get off the roller coaster. I didn't owe anyone any money, and so I simply told the Colombians that I quit.

Around this time, my cousin's daughter Faye died. Nickie was not able to attend the service, so I went alone. As I sat in church that day listening to Bishop Wally speak about life and God, I began to feel different in some undefined way. Finally, I put my finger on it—the Holy Spirit had touched me and from that day on my life would change.

Though I had seen so many people die, it never occurred to me that I could die too. I realized that I didn't want my children living with the burden of knowing I was the victim of an assassin who wanted my money. In that moment I realized that my life meant more to me than all the material things I possessed. I wanted to live—to be a good father and husband, and all of these feelings were washing over me with a force that could only be described as divine guidance.

When I shared the news with Nickie, she was so excited. She relished the idea of her husband coming home to her. She'd always wanted a family with close ties; she had wanted us to attend church together and be a family in the eyes of the Lord. I wanted to attend Bishop Wally's church but told her if that was not the church she usually attended she should stay with her own. "Jerry," Nickie happily said, "just as long as we all attend church, it doesn't matter which church you go to."

That Sunday I drove to my church with my wife and son driving in a car behind me, on the way to their church. As they passed me, they smiled and waved, and I felt so powerful in some new and undefined way. As I entered Bishop Wally's church I stood and watched everyone. Suddenly, I felt a nudge from behind and when I turned, my wife and son were standing behind me. My first thought was that Nickie didn't trust me—for good reason. She flashed her big smile and explained, "You know this is my church too." She gave me a hug and said, "I am so happy that we are finally together in this newfound life."

I felt terrible knowing I had been so lost in my own world that I didn't even know what church my wife and son had been attending. They say God works in mysterious ways, and I now do believe that. Nickie's prayers were for us to attend the same church as a family and that happened. It was no coincidence. I told her I wanted God in my life and needed his blessing and grace, not just for that day but for every day. For the first time, I truly regretted the life I had been living.

Services that day were splendid and everyone was so welcoming. My family ate breakfast together for the first time in a long while. That day, as I began this new life with the Lord, I couldn't help feeling the pressure in my mind. Although this life felt wonderful, I knew it was going to fall down around me and I was prepared for it.

At the time I started going to church I didn't know my last two years were now on Memorex. Everything I said or that someone said to me was all recorded by the Feds. Everyone I loved was being scrutinized. The clouds were again over me and they were darker than I could ever remember. I didn't want to face the truth alone and was so thankful the Lord was in my corner, finally. I had been an extremely angry and violent person, but now my life had been transformed by the power of Jesus Christ.

After my spiritual recommitment to Jesus Christ, and while I was carrying around real fears of a federal investigation, serious family issues dominated my attention. In 1997, my older sister Mary Ann was being treated for an ulcer. Her rapid weight loss prompted a second opinion, and she was diagnosed with cancer. Having been misdiagnosed originally, the cancer was now in the later stages. Once she was diagnosed her health declined quickly, both mentally and physically. She was so worried about her children, wondering who would take care of them. This was the least of her problems; we were a close-knit family and no one's children would ever suffer.

Having been in prison so much of my early life, I had never been particularly close to Mary Ann, but now that I was free, I wanted to be the tower of power for her and my family. As the cancer progressed, her last wish was to see her oldest son, Ernest, who had been in prison the last six years. Her doctor explained that if she went to sleep it would be forever, and so I held her in my arms working hard to keep her awake. The prison warden offered Ernest the choice of being with her as she was dying or going to the funeral. Ernest loved his mother deeply and he wanted to be with her as long as she was with us.

It was a long four hours until the prison van arrived at Momma's house. I spent the whole time holding Mary Ann and pleading with her to hold on, that Ernest would be here any minute. When he arrived he was devastated to see her condition. He had not seen his mother for two years and during that time she had lost over a hundred pounds. He burst into tears, falling to his knees and crying over her. I helped him to the bed so he could lie beside his mother and hold her. For four hours he never left her side, but then prison called and Ernest had to leave. I never wanted to let go of Mary Ann that day. I wanted to stop her pain, to change things somehow, to make her well. But I wasn't a god with those kinds of powers, and so I eventually quit talking. I kissed her goodbye, as did the rest of the family, and let her slip into her life with the Lord.

The alarm went off and I reflexively leapt out of bed, sweat dripping from my face. God, what a nightmare—Denise had called to tell me the Feds had kicked in her door and that everyone I knew was facing the same fate. The winds of fear ripped through my stomach. I looked over and saw that Nickie was sleeping peacefully, so I quietly slid out of bed, careful not to awaken her. I ran the bathtub hot to help me battle this horrible feeling. Federal agents in my dreams, doing what they did best—wreaking havoc in my life. I felt as if I were spinning straight down and off a bridge, with everyone I knew hurtling below me, all of us heading directly to hell. Everything felt so real and I kept telling myself it was only a dream, but I didn't want my loved ones to be hurt—or worse, end up in prison for something I had done. Finally, I got dressed and bent down to kiss Nickie goodbye, but I stopped, not wanting to wake her, and I was not yet ready to talk about all that was bothering me. I jumped into my car and started calling everyone I knew to make sure they were all right. Everyone was fine, and I relaxed a bit. It had just been a nightmare.

It was June when the light of the Lord found me, and I knew I was doing the wrong thing. It was an easy life to live except for the steady fear of being caught. This is when I quit the drug trafficking business for good. The pressure of living in the fast world of drug running was over and I wanted to forget it forever. I had a beautiful house, two fine cars, and a new swimming pool. I also owned a liquor store and was on the verge of opening another business. I wanted to be a good businessman, and even though I had no formal education, I wanted to provide a good life for my entire family. My preacher, Wally, guided me toward the path I should be following, and I began to work toward that goal every day.

As I searched for a warehouse to house equipment for my second business, the wind churning in my stomach grew more and more intense. Although I had quit selling drugs, the Feds hadn't stopped tracking me. Back then I was not aware of how the federal system worked; the only case I had been involved with was a state murder case.

I arrived home early one night, something I was not able

to do often. I put the kids to bed and then simply tried to relax, but I was restless and unable to settle. Around four in the morning, I finally drifted off, only to be awakened by my beeper. At first I tried to ignore it, but the feeling growing in my stomach made me check the number. It was the burglar alarm company who informed me that the alarm on the Hermens Street residence—Denise's home—was going off. As I drove to the house, my heart was pounding. I wanted to believe it was a random break-in but could tell immediately that this was far more than an ordinary robbery. Where there had been an entrance door to the residence, there was now a piece of plywood. The security bars on the windows had been removed and thrown into the front yard. The once-serene home in one of New Orleans's upscale neighborhoods looked as if a bomb had gone off within it. The walls were torn out and the ceiling, attic, and all the new furniture were thrown into the middle of the room. I was grateful that Denise and our daughter, Ivory, had spent the night with Denise's mother and had been spared the trauma of watching their home be destroyed.

I found the search warrant on the kitchen counter—the only thing in the house still standing. Clearly, the Feds had been responsible for the catastrophic destruction.

The wind had now turned into a full-blown storm. Standing in the middle of the mess, I called my lawyer to explain that Denise had nothing to do with anything I had been involved in. I left in a daze, heading to Denise's mother's house to share what had happened, when my beeper went off again. This number I recognized as my sister Maxine's but could not understand why she would be calling so early in the morning. I talked to my nephew, Brian, who was also watching his beautiful house being destroyed. The Feds had called everyone out of the house and then went to work. My body turned numb; I could not feel anything but knew the Feds would be coming for me next.

Brian was the first casualty of the war the Feds were waging against my family and friends. They arrested him for a drug purchase they had set up. The bills were marked, so he must have sold something. My heart was in my throat, but I tried to pull myself together to post bond for Brian. Each bondsman I spoke to was skeptical that a bond would be set, given that Brian's was a federal offense. They were correct. When Brian was finally able to call me, he confirmed what I already knew—the Feds were coming after me for reasons unknown to him. I told him I already knew.

The next day I went to work as usual. About noon, Salazar, my Colombian friend, came to visit me at the liquor store. Nickie was working out front while I was in my office. I could hear their conversation. He was interested in why I hadn't contacted him in a while. Nickie shared that I had gotten out of the business and didn't want anything to do with them or the drug business. So he left, only to return a couple of hours later with a friend. This time I talked with him and the conversation wasn't pleasant. I told him what had happened with the Feds and asked him to understand my position. I also asked if he thought it might be time for him to get out of the business as well. He commented that they were Colombians and this was a way of life for them. They would not be stopping. I again reiterated that it was no longer my way of life. After they left, I locked up the store and drove home.

As I approached the house, I noticed a dark sedan parked nearby. The windows were tinted so I couldn't see anyone but knew the Feds were watching my house. An hour later, I came out and got into my pickup truck in case they decided to arrest me then. As I drove away, they followed me back to the liquor store, where I parked my truck out front. After I opened and re-closed the store, they were still there, waiting to follow me wherever I went. I drove home with them following me. They stayed outside until after darkness fell. I knew it was time for them to make a move, and at about four a.m., they knocked on the door.

Nickie woke up asking who could be banging on the door at this time of the morning, and I told her it was the Feds and that they were here to take me in. Hoping to keep the door from being destroyed, I went to open it. Along the way I picked up my daughter, Isis, who was crying. I opened the door and for the second time in my life was staring at a half-dozen weapons pointed at me, this time with laser spots visible on my chest. They were pushing me and screaming for me to drop my child. Very calmly I told them I would not drop my child, and then a female agent stepped up and grabbed Isis out of my arms. At that point they all jumped me, pushed me around till I was facing the wall, and cuffed me.

The huge light shining in my face was also lighting up the whole front of my house. I had known they were coming and I was not resisting. In fact, I told them this could all happen in a more civil way, but they weren't interested in any way but their own. Then they tore up my home just as they had done to Denise's and Brian's. I asked them not to go into my son's room with their guns drawn, but they didn't listen to me. They had no respect whatsoever. I wasn't wearing a shirt, and so when it was time to leave, one agent yelled upstairs to another to throw down a shirt for me. Within a second or two, one of Nickie's thongs sailed over the rail into the room, followed by an order for me to "put that on." Although I could not see them, I was sure my neighbors could see me.

My mind was racing during the long drive to the Federal Building. When we arrived they took me to the second floor, and when the door opened my heart sank. There were no Colombians there as I had anticipated. Later I found out they had been arrested in Las Vegas and Texas. The room was filled with friends and family: Denise; Hazel; Corneal, along with his wife, Dewanna; Brian and his girlfriend, Rozenia; Lenny's sister, Lenjan; Donald Bugish; and my uncle Frederick. Now Nickie and I joined them and the guilt was indescribable. These were all people who trusted me, and I had let them down. They were all charged with conspiracy to distribute cocaine. My worst nightmare was being played out, and my first urge was to try to help the people in the room who weren't involved in anything I had done.

"Conspiracy" cast a wide net and included anyone who knew or was in any manner associated with selling cocaine. The Feds reported that they had 306 kilos of cocaine in their possession and the Colombians had said it was mine. Months ago it could have been mine, but at that moment I was no longer working with the Colombians in any manner, and so I told them clearly that the cocaine was not mine. The Colombians were lying to cover their own asses.

"You're not going to cooperate with us?" the Feds asked.

"No," I said. "You'll have to talk to my lawyers about that."

After the gathering, everyone was held in custody. After about two weeks, Bugish made a deal to identify voices on the taped recordings the Feds had made in exchange for bail. Nickie, Denise, and Hazel knew that if they talked, I would be sent back to prison for the rest of my life. They were told that if they pleaded guilty it would help me and so they took the plea deal that allowed them to post bail. I could breathe easier knowing that they were at least somewhat free. There was no bond for me. I would have to sit tight knowing that only a miracle would allow me to walk out of jail. This time I had the power of prayer, and as I waited sixteen months for a court date, I said more prayers than I had in the previous thirty-six years of my life.

When I was released from prison the first time, I swore that nothing could ever put me back in that place. The nightmares were the hardest thing to deal with. I would wake thinking I was somewhere else but then realize I was right back in jail. At that moment in time, my life was all about material things, and all the things I owned would now go to the government. And it wasn't hard to imagine that I would be seeing my beautiful children only at some visiting room in a federal prison. I tried not to think of all the people I had hurt. My misery stretched my emotions to the breaking point. The only way to stay positive was to turn to prayer—it was all I had.

The Feds had built a tight case against me. The wiretaps and

Bugish's voice identification sealed the case. The Feds were sure that everyone else they had arrested would plead out to make it easier for themselves. Brian and I were the only holdouts, both preferring to wait for a court date and a trial. The Feds had the case on one hand and the Colombians on the other hand telling them that I was the "main man." And as fate would have it, they would hang the "Kingpin" status on me, which meant I could potentially get another life sentence if convicted.

The last life sentence I received at seventeen was a set-up, this one I brought on myself. But having a life sentence in Angola had done nothing to prepare me for the real world. In fact, there were no educational opportunities for men in Angola when the sentence is life without parole. Training us for anything was deemed a waste of resources. Our only value was in picking cotton or working the fields that helped to keep the prison working. In that environment you either became a killer or perfected your ability to scrub floors. It did not leave much room for thought.

When I was released the first time and trying to build a boxing career, I held a number of menial jobs for minimum wage and no future. Spending over a decade of my life in prison, where authority was used punitively to control inmates, made listening to a boss extremely challenging. I bounced from job to job. Entering the drug business didn't hold much of a future either, but it did allow me to help so many people that had so little. It was a thrill to give generously to schools and churches. My family didn't want for anything, and the kids in the projects where I had grown up loved to see my pickup truck coming into the neighborhood. All anyone had to do was ask.

The Assistant United States Attorney showed my attorney, Michael Lawrence, a list of people who were willing to testify against me. I was not shown the list so I had no way of knowing who would or would not talk. I feared that the list could have anyone on it, even people who weren't involved in my case. That had happened once in my life. Anyone who knew my name could try to make deals on it. So I told my attorney not to accept their deal. The Feds had said all they were going to say and so had I—we were at a standoff. Being the smart guys that they are, they brought in a secret weapon to break me down—my momma, accompanied by Mr. Lawrence. This was a smart move because they knew the love and respect I had for Momma. She said if I got another life sentence, she wouldn't be able to wait that long, but if I pleaded guilty and received a shorter sentence, she could see another miracle happening. She asked me to plead guilty so I could someday leave prison and spend the rest of my life with my family and children. She cried through the whole visit, and I could feel her strong love for me. Again I was behind a screen and unable to hold her or even touch the hand of this woman who had guided me through so many years of life. Then and there I decided to take the plea. I would be looking at twelve to fourteen years. In the back of my mind I knew someone still owed me thirteen years for the past unjust conviction. I was hoping for a miracle.

Mr. Lawrence returned later to tell me that the plea would happen the way I wanted it to and that the three women in my life—Nickie, Denise, and Hazel—would be able to take care of my children.

In the long run, each of these women suffered for what I had done. When I was dealing, Hazel became like an answering service for me. Not purposely, but I was in the habit of not answering my phone, so I eventually gave her number out so she could call or beep me with important calls. I hung around Hazel's house often when I felt pressured. She was always cooking for me and giving me a shoulder to cry on. If I didn't answer my pages, people would start calling everywhere to find me. The Feds recorded Hazel telling me that a man with a Spanish accent was trying to call me. That was enough to charge her with conspiracy—she ended up getting three years' probation.

Nickie was between a rock and a hard place. Being my wife complicated her life, but she was also living my dream. I had never told her about my level of involvement in drug dealing, and she was not aware of the details of my activities. She just needed enough money to shop. However, telling the Feds that she knew nothing at all would have been a lie. Ultimately, she was booked on a lesser charge of "misprision," which carried a potential six to twelve months in prison. She ended up getting six months in a halfway house.

Denise was drawn in because she had called me one day while I was traveling to Texas. The conversation was taped by the Feds, and when she asked me where I was going and why, I told her I would tell her when I returned. I never did tell her anything about the trip to Texas, but the Feds did not believe that. They were used to lies and simply assumed that her denial was a lie. She, too, was charged with "misprision" and received six months in camp, six months in boot camp, and another six months in a halfway house. I will always carry a heavy burden for having dragged these three women into my mistakes.

Lenny's sister, Lenjan, was the other woman recorded talking with me. In our conversations we actually discussed drug business. She was stopped in LaPlace, Texas, and arrested. She is currently serving out a seven-year sentence in Texas that could have been substantially reduced by pleading out and talking with the Feds. She didn't, and in this field, that is considered honorable.

And then it came down to me. I pleaded guilty to having 150 kilos of cocaine and was sentenced to twenty years in federal prison. My son, Isaac, refused to smile after I was sentenced, as he was now without a father in his day-to-day life. I grew up without a father, as did my brothers and sisters. We knew that if anything went wrong the only person to help would be Momma, and I give thanks to God every night for the gift he has given me through my mother's love and support and for my children, Iris, Isaac, Ivory, and Isis.

18

PRISON AGAIN

Isaac Knapper

In the summer of 2000, I arrived at the Federal Correctional Institution, Yazoo City, Mississippi, after serving a little over a year of my twenty-year sentence for drug trafficking. Yazoo was a "medium high" security prison but I had nothing to fear. My uncle Frederick "Fox" had arrived three months before me and had shared my reputation as a fighter, and this reputation meant that no one dared to mess with me. Period. There was nothing for me to prove. Few of the other inmates had been through what I had at that point in my life, and therefore the coveted quality of respect had been imputed from day one.

This time around, "respect" had a different meaning for me, different because I had changed. When I was sent to Angola, I was an innocent young man placed in a jungle. I was violent, aggressive, and angry. At Angola I earned respect through years of winning one physical altercation after another. However, in Yazoo I was sentenced for a crime I had committed, and that made a significant difference in how I approached doing my time. I needed to take responsibility for my actions. Having established a relationship with God after my release from Angola, I was better equipped to deal with prison the second time around.

By far the biggest influence in changing my attitude was the relationship I had built with my momma, who had lived through a hell on earth, yet never lost her faith or confidence in God and the Bible. Between prison sentences, I had spent as much time as possible with my momma, and during this time the things she had tried to teach me finally began to make sense. She was my hero and always would be, and I wanted to be like her in so many ways. I needed to change, and that change meant transforming my identity from the "predator" that once roamed the cell blocks of Angola, ready to hurt or even kill for the slightest infraction, to a "protector" of the weaker inmates who found themselves targets of the bullies and shake-down artists who patrolled the dorms and cells of FCI Yazoo.

My relationship with Caesar Brown illustrated my change in attitude after I found Jesus and took accountability for my actions. I first met Caesar in 2003 when he was transferred to Yazoo from Beaumont Federal Prison in Texas. Caesar had made headlines in the New Orleans newspapers as Governor Ed Edward's right-hand man. Caesar had been convicted of bribery related to the selling of illegal riverboat casino licenses and was sentenced to ten years in federal prison.

When he arrived at Yazoo his high profile made him a high-priority shakedown target for the more hardened convicts. Two inmates, Chi-Town, a large African American man, and another guy from the Barrio Azteca's gang were extorting Caesar by giving him commissary slips each week with items they wanted him to purchase for them. Caesar had originally sought me out because we were both from Louisiana, and in federal prison, people from the same state tend to stick together. When I learned of the extortion I was extremely upset, particularly since they were giving him lists so long that he had no money left over to buy anything for himself. He shared that the shakedowns had been going on for three weeks. He protested when I asked him to give me the slips so I could take care of it, but he finally relented.

With the two neatly folded commissary slips in my hand, I walked down the hall, headed for Chi-Town's living quarters. As I walked all I could think of was my mother praying for me while I was in Angola and visiting me every week for those thirteen long years. I also thought of how, after my release from Angola, she told me that God had uniquely gifted me with talents and that I needed to start using my gifts for others instead of myself.

When I found Chi-Town, I handed him the commissary slips and asked if he had seen these. He was stunned and nervous, even though he was a good five inches taller than me. He apologized, saying he did not realize that Caesar was my home-boy, but before he could say more, I insisted, "Never again do you go to Caesar for anything." After he assured me that he wouldn't, I walked back to my unit to give Caesar the good news. My heart was flooded with warm feelings. I was no longer a predator; I was a protector of the weak—and Momma would have been so proud of me. For the first time in my life it was important to me that I pleased and served others, not just myself.

The story did not end there. About three weeks later, Caesar told me that the Mexican gang member had been pressing him with commissary slips again. This time I walked to the Spanish TV room, despite Caesar's protests that I would get hurt given all the men in there. Caesar's guess of twenty-five men in the TV room was close—twenty-one men were glued to the television set bolted into the wall. When I arrived, I immediately turned off the TV set—more for shock value than anything else. I asked who spoke English and Spanish and asked one guy to come forward to translate what I was about to say.

As he was coming up to translate, I grabbed the Mexican gang member out of his chair, threw him up against the wall, and held him there by his throat. No one moved. Through the translator I spoke: "If any one of you boys ever hands Caesar another commissary list, I will do a whole lot worse than this." I threw the man to the ground and placed my foot on his throat for effect. No one said a word and no one moved. No one wanted to risk bodily harm over a commissary slip, and each man knew that if a brawl broke out, they might win but not before eight of the twenty-one guys were badly injured. That was not a price any of them were willing to pay.

While I was incarcerated at Yazoo, I had the opportunity to talk with young people who visited the prison in one of many "scared straight" programs. This was another way that I could give back. I would tell them that "I am doing time so they won't have to." In other words, all they had to do was to listen to me, identify the pitfalls that had snared me, and be vigilant about avoiding them themselves.

By 2012 I had served fourteen years of my sentence and much had changed. My wife, Nickie, asked for a divorce, which was not a surprise. I wanted to support her in whatever decisions she made for herself. She is a terrific mother to our two children, Isaac III and Isis, and she is still the funniest person I have ever met. She has the ability to mimic anyone, and I swear, the practical jokes we shared will continue to provide me with a lifetime of smiles. As I have grown and taken responsibility for my actions, I am more aware than ever of the pain I have brought to her life from my past infidelities. Denise, too, has been free for many years and has remained supportive every step of this journey. She is a wonderful mother to Ivory and Ricquel, my daughters, and she is still the sweet person I fell in love with many years ago in the lab. She visited me every chance she could and brought her kindness, respect, and love. I would humbly kneel in front of her with a bowl of water and cloth and proceed to wash her feet as I tell her how sorry I am for all the pain and suffering I have caused her through the years.

After serving fifteen years of my twenty-year sentence I began the slow transition out of prison life and into the free world by being sent to the Federal Correctional Complex in Pollack, Louisiana. Though Pollack has a high-security prison, I was transferred to its minimum-security satellite camp on the grounds. The camp did not have the high perimeter fences standard in higher-security institutions and inmates stayed in dormitories rather than cells. The biggest benefit of the move was that I was now closer to my family—it is just a three- to four-hour drive from New Orleans to the facility located in north central Louisiana, in the Kisatchie National Forest. I stayed in the camp for one year and then was sent to a halfway house on June 1, 2015. This was my first real taste of freedom. Here I was able to work and visit home on the weekends. In fact, while I was still living in the halfway house, Denise and I were married in September of 2015.

Being released from prison the second time was even more emotional than the first. In 1992 when I was released from Angola, I was still a young man with a life ahead of me and no responsibilities. But when I returned to prison in 2000, I left behind a wife and children. I had missed so much of their lives. By the time I was released to the halfway house I had four grown children and a family of my own to reconnect with. I had to learn how to have adult relationships without the structure of the prison directing my moves. And I had to form relationships with my now grown children who knew me only from brief visits to the prison through the years. They never had a chance to know me as a man and a father. And I needed to get to know them, having missed every major milestone of their lives. I was a biological father, a stranger from another place. Getting to know them was not easy, as none of them are big talkers. The relationships are still growing.

There is no doubt that almost thirty years of my life in prison has taken its toll. When I was released after my second imprisonment, I immediately noticed that being in crowds of people left me feeling anxious and shaky until I could train myself to relax and be comfortable with other people. I have nightmares and flashbacks to some of the rougher moments in prison, and at times I find myself depressed and anxious. And while I never worry that I will do something wrong or illegal again, in the back of my mind there is always a gnawing worry that I will be accused again of doing something I didn't do. That feeling is particularly intense being on parole because it is so easy to get a violation. Fortunately, I have a lovely probation officer, Nicole, who is actually supportive and not just out to pin violations on me.

19

Seventeen Again

Amy Banks

On paper it appears that my siblings and I have created success-ful lives despite the early death of our father. Our accomplish-ments are a reflection of my parents' relentless belief in the importance of a good education. As a child, I remember hear-ing my friends moan about Sunday mornings spent fidgeting in a church pew, and as an adult there have been times I longed to tether myself to a spiritual belief larger than myself; but the ritual of church was not a part of our lives growing up. Our religion was books, newspapers, and spirited debates. Sunday mornings were spent hanging out at home while my father read the *New York Times* and watched *Meet the Press* and *Face the Nation* back to back. We lived in a modest split-level ranch, a little tight for the six of us, and our dining room table was usually covered with blue books and yellow paper tablets. It was my father's home office where he wrote books, graded tests, and organized lectures amidst the chaos of his family.

My parents were teachers by training and demeanor and preached their belief that a good education could overcome any obstacle in life. My father was living proof. Having grown up fatherless with a mother who worked as a domestic, there is no doubt that earning his doctorate in history improved his station in life. His children have followed in his footsteps, earning advanced degrees from some of the top colleges and universities on the East Coast—Columbia, Wellesley, Tufts, Harvard, Northeastern, NYU, and Georgetown. Through the lens of education, we are a successful group.

But just below the surface we each carry scars from our fa-ther's murder. Hypervigilance and a lack of trust in the world have worn us down emotionally and physically. Traumatic events too overwhelming for a person's mind to comprehend can trigger the body's alarm signals so often that the body itself becomes the danger. Like an animal caught in a trap that chews off its own leg to escape, our bodies have turned on each of us in a confused bid to destroy the element that is carrying the threat. Education could not protect us from this fate.

Over a period of time, stress wears down the human body. Initially, cortisol levels rise to temper the chronic stimulation of the fight-or-flight stress response. However, when post-traumatic stress disorder sets in, as it did with my brother, the chronic replaying of the traumatic event leads to chronically elevated cortisol levels that eventually become toxic to the brain and body. At some point, after months or years, there is a tipping point at which the elevated cortisol levels begin to wear down the immune system, opening the door to a variety of diseases.

Like many people, my brother tried his best to medicate his adrenalized system with alcohol, and this strategy of drinking himself into numbness and oblivion came close to killing him a dozen times. His weakened system eventually snapped under the strain, and he developed an autoimmune disease—in his case, multiple sclerosis—a condition in which the body literally turns on itself in protest. He has been in grave condition many times over the last twenty years and the impact has trickled down to me and my sisters; we exist in a state of hypervigilance and increased fear and worry knowing that his body can only take so much, and that we could very well get another call or knock on the door—an echo of our father's early death.

Kate was diagnosed with chronic fatigue syndrome in her early twenties when twitching and spasms wracked her body. She now reacts to many of life's insults in the extreme. She developed allergies and sensitivities she did not have as a child and eventually left the fast-paced, stressful life in the U.S. for a more controlled existence in Europe. Recently, she was diagnosed with rheumatoid arthritis, an autoimmune disease where her body turns on itself, misidentifying tissue in her joints and organs as foreign and mounting an attack on them.

And in 2005 my life was hijacked a second time. This time the bullet was a small offending clump of malignant cells on the surface of an ovary, lying in wait to rob my children of their mother too early. I had no bloating, no gas, no gastrointestinal symptoms of any kind. In fact, I was forty-three years old, with a loving partner and beloved children. I exercised at least six times a week and rarely drank. My biggest vice was Diet Coke.

My greatest wish for my children has been for them to emerge from childhood with their family intact. That desire pushed me to consult with a genetic oncologist about my cancer risk given my strong family history. She asked directly, "What would you do if you found out you had a genetic mutation for breast and ovarian cancer?" My answer was clear and immediate. "Remove both my breasts and ovaries to decrease the risk." The 90 percent chance of developing breast cancer and 50 percent chance of ovarian cancer were simply too high. The blood test was drawn in February, the positive results were shared with me in April, and in May I was on an operating room table as the very organs that made me a woman and a mother were removed. Two nights before the surgery my partner and I made love, gently, lovingly, in a tearful good-bye to these organs that would never again be part of the intimacy we shared. And after the good-byes, I "got on with it," clear in my belief that this was not the worst thing that had happened to me.

Two weeks later, while still recuperating from the surgeries and proud of having regained full range of motion in my arms, my surgeon called with the shocking news that the microscopic examination of my tissue showed cancer on the surface of an ovary and within a fallopian tube. Two sites. Though it was caught in an early stage there was still the war ahead—a second operation where I was gutted like a fish, my uterus and omentum removed and an aggressive search done deep in my pelvis for lymph nodes that might be harboring more cancer. And then six months of chemotherapy designed to track down the one or two cells that might have entered my bloodstream traveling to a distant site to set up a new community of cancer cells.

I was stunned by the news and tried to call my partner, then my sister, and when I could not reach either I called my sister-in-law, Liz, the mother of six and an Episcopal minister. She was calm and kind and offered just the right amount of support to get me through the afternoon. I began to settle into the idea that at forty-three years old I was starting a fight for my life. Any idea of protecting my children from the early losses, the fear and anxiety of my childhood, were tossed.

Both my sisters were tested. Mercifully, Kate tested negative. However, Nancy was also positive and shortly after I finished chemotherapy, the peach fuzz on my head providing little protection from the New England winter, I traveled to New York to be by her side when she awoke from her own mastectomies in excruciating pain. After months of healing, Nancy and I both felt we had dodged a bullet.

The fact that we are all still standing is a tribute to my mother's absolute love of life. As she lay in her bedroom during the last weeks of her life, she repeatedly kicked out the hospice workers, stating clearly that she was not going to spend the rest of her life talking about death—with anyone! I had so many questions I wanted to ask her. Was she afraid of dying? Did she think she would be reunited with Dad? Could I reach her on the other side? She would have no part of it. She wanted to talk about life, not death. She wanted to hear what her kids were doing in the world, the conversations we were having with friends, the plans we were making for the future. She made it clear to all of us that Helena Thelma Poland Banks was going to say goodbye by honoring life up till the very moment of her death. That spark burns in each of us.

The long-term emotional scars from my father's murder are less apparent but can also be crippling. My mother's collapse set in motion a complicated relational template in me that survives to this day—the unwavering belief that it is my job to "fix" other people's pain. It is a 24/7 task and unconsciously, I was drawn to people and places where the pain was extreme.

During my third year of medical school I was the most junior member of a surgical team at DC General Hospital, an inner-city hospital located beside the prison. Like many city hospitals, DC General was underfunded and overutilized, its beds largely filled with African American people suffering the ill effects of poverty and social neglect—an epidemic of diabetes, emphysema, drug addiction, and violence. This was the late eighties and the southwest quadrant of DC was in the midst of massive drug wars. Practicing medicine in this environment was like drinking water through a fire hose.

Once the sun went down, the shooting began and the emergency room would fill with patients. By midnight the sound of sirens was steady as ambulances rushed to the ER, carrying young men who were establishing territory and getting revenge, men who were shooting and dying. I needed to be there like an alcoholic needs a bottle of booze; needed to see the fatal gunshot wounds in the chests and the heads. I learned that red blood clotting on the rear end of blue denim was not an attempted murder but a warning shot designed to humiliate a rival gang member. The victim would survive but with a colostomy, "a bag," they called it on the street; their feces would now slither out of a hole in the abdomen. Too often, in an attempt to fire a shot in the buttocks or the intestines, the spine would be hit and those boys would leave the hospital paralyzed, in a wheelchair for the rest of their lives, their manhood, dignity, and power stolen. I felt strangely at home in this world with a deep compassion for these young men caught up in raw violence.

My surgical team was on call every third night, which meant I would arrive at the hospital at six a.m. one day and go home around seven p.m. the following day—thirty-six hours later. We were all on our feet working for the entire thirty-six hours. For me the most difficult time would be between about three and four a.m.—regardless of how many Diet Cokes I drank. My colleagues could catch a few minutes of sleep between pages in the call room or even put their heads down at the nurses' station and grab ten minutes, but I never could. I was a bad sleeper before my father's murder, and after that, falling asleep was a nightmare—literally.

One memorable night my pager went off at two a.m. calling me to the operating room stat—a nineteen-year-old boy was in the ER with a gunshot wound to the back of his leg. Right away I could tell this was serious, as his lower leg was already swollen into a large blue balloon. His popliteal artery had been severed and each heartbeat sent more blood into his calf. If it was not treated immediately the pressure from the swelling would eventually collapse the surrounding vessels and blood flow to his leg would stop. Many young men left the hospital with amputations for this reason.

My job was crucial and tedious. For six hours I was to put pressure upstream on the groin, to block the blood flow to the lower leg so that the chief resident could dissect the artery in a clean surgical field. I was bone tired, and as the surgery proceeded slowly, meticulously, I eventually dozed off, waking to the sound of the chief resident screaming at me, his dissection area now filled with warm blood. This created a welcome jolt of adrenaline—enough to keep me awake for another fifteen minutes, and then the whole thing would happen again. There were no other bodies to step in to do my job, and everyone else was also running on fumes. This job, to stem the flow of the hemorrhage, is so essential, so constant, and, I now recognize, so me. Since the day my father was murdered there has been no moment to rest, to stop, to sleep, to take a nap. Nap, Knapper, father, murder, death.

After medical school I chose to specialize in psychiatry, and for the last two decades I have worked in the emotional emergency department of life. Each person's story is unique—sexual abuse as a child, rape as an adult. I have worked with refugees fleeing genocide, parents whose children have been murdered, men and women fleeing domestic violence, survivors of the Boston Marathon bombing and the 9/11 terrorist attacks.

One client I work with, a tremendous success in every socially accepted way, has a pain so deep and so isolated from human comfort that when it emerges, she doubles over and turns ashen. Early in our work together she described her primary way of coping with this pain: velocitizing. I recognized it immediately. The fiercest emotional pain has the power to swallow you whole if you are stationary long enough. With laser focus and Herculean stamina, one can hover along a plane of what looks to the outside world like maximum functioning and appear remarkably accomplished. The fear of sinking into the quicksand of grief and terror fuels the velocity. Wake up, plan the day, make lists, check off when you have done something on your list, plan a trip, plan dinner, book the trip, buy stuff for the dinner you have planned, make the dinner, think about breakfast while you are eating dinner, book clients, see more clients, exercise, a lot, volunteer at your kids' schools, coach their teams, play on your own team. There is no end to the creativity of velocitizing. It is the anti-meditation. Some would say this is proof that I need meditation, but for those of us who simply know that their grief and terror are bigger than they are, the idea of sitting still and inviting those emotions to the surface is akin to cage diving with great white sharks—without the cage.

Over the years, I wondered how Isaac survived in prison for twelve years without the ability to escape. A life laid out in front of him with nothing but time to feel the pain of being falsely accused of murder; to ruminate on the fact that his skin color and address made him invisible and interchangeable with any five-foot-nine-inch Black teenager from the projects of New Orleans. In the New Orleans legal system, his Black life did not matter. Though my psychiatric training told me emotional pains cannot and should not be compared, I couldn't help myself. His loss felt bigger and more complicated than my own, and I wondered how he survived those twelve years trapped in hell. I wondered if he had faith, if he found some mental and physical comfort in prayer. I had read that he was a boxer and perhaps that was his version of velocitizing. Had he boxed to stay alive, to get through the boredom of every day or in the belief that he would leave Angola? I wondered. As the years ticked by, I was drawn to Isaac and I did not know why.

After cancer and Hurricane Katrina another ten years passed. Phil continued to struggle with drinking, eventually moving back to his childhood home in Brewer, Maine to live with his girlfriend. Kate moved from Rome to Monaco to raise her two boys and continued to write children's books. Her own health challenges led her to study energy medicine, and she started a successful practice as an intuitive healer. After graduating from Columbia University with her PhD in history, Nancy decided to pass on a university academic career, feeling she simply "liked her life too much" to be under the perpetual pressure of chasing a tenure-track position. She found a job and a second home in a progressive, private high school in the Bronx where she is now the director of student programs, a history teacher, and a beloved mentor. My partner, Judy, and I and the kids moved to Lexington where we could raise Jayme and Alex in a loving and safe community.

Time is distorted when a person loses a parent or child prematurely. The seamless, predictable cadence of life bifurcates into before and after, all future events remembered in relation to that one tragic moment in time. By the time I was fifty-three years old, my adult life had been punctuated by milestones referenced to the day my father was killed. My thirty-fourth birthday was a pivot point marking the moment in time when I had been alive with him as long as without him. My three-dimensional life with him reduced to two dimensions. As the years passed by, I felt the once fluid memories of our interactions replaced by stagnant photographs of him, snapshots that would flash before my mind trailed by a wave of sadness. Each day of my forty-fifth year I held a visceral awareness that he had been my age when he was murdered. He seemed so old at the time of his death, but at forty-five I had eight-year-old twins, a medical career just taking off, and a new appreciation of just how young he had been when he was killed and how much we had all lost when he died.

And then 2015 came along and my children turned seventeen, the same age I was when my father was murdered and the same age Isaac was when he was sent to Angola for the rest of his life. I had not anticipated what that would feel like. At their age, I had become frozen by the events in New Orleans, so the emotional impact of this particular birthday took me by surprise. Back when Jayme and Alex were still in single digits, Judy and I often discussed the challenges of raising teenagers. She had spent her junior and senior years of high school at a boarding school desperately homesick. I was dismissive of her concerns about the children's well-being, filling in the gaps of my own emotional memory of that time with exciting new possibilities for the kids. I was in denial about the way those years had been stolen by my father's murder and had no idea my absence of fear was a reflection of so much numbness.

As a trauma therapist I was intellectually aware of the risks posed by having your child become the same age you were when a trauma happened. But I had no idea what that would feel like. As my children neared seventeen their very beings became a constant reminder of that painful time. I felt my own vulnerability as I watched Alex's body become long and lean with muscles popping and fuzz growing along the line of his now square jaw. My heart ached as I watched Jayme grow into a young woman with a full chest and confident stride. As the date of Jayme and Alex's seventeenth birthday approached, sadness bubbled from the deepest part of me. As the days passed by, the feelings expanded; they filled my stomach with a knot and my chest with an ache, and then stuck directly in my throat.

They were walking, breathing reminders of how young and vulnerable Isaac and I had been. Some days they seemed like babies as they tried to make their way through this awkward stage—equal parts dependence and independence. I watched them with such grace, humility, and appreciation for the safety in which they were being raised. And as I watched, it was clear that I could no longer hold my grief back. The massive steel wall I had erected within myself was beginning to crack and I simply knew I had two choices: to actively participate in dismantling this wall or to be buried alive as it crumbled around me, leaving me forever stuck within the emotional rubble. Quite frankly, both choices felt impossible.

20

CONFRONTING THE BEAST

Amy Banks

Every summer our family spends a couple of weeks in Pennsylvania on a private lake preserve founded in the Quaker spirit of serenity, simplicity, and service. This is a tradition straight from my partner, Judy's, family, and as she walks the common areas where groups congregate at the dining hall, the art room, or the tennis courts she sees the faces of her own childhood friends in their children and grandchildren. It is simple time spent boating, sunning, making s'mores, and visiting with family. To me our time at the preserve, known as PLP, is an oasis. Because it carries the familiar sights, smells, and sounds of Judy's childhood, not my own, it is one of the few places in my life untarnished by associations with my father's murder.

Miles of dirt roads wind through dense green forests, and emerald ferns circle the lake. Through the years I've developed a routine of riding my bike along these roads, fast and intense, equal parts exercise and meditation, the smells blending with the fresh air to clean my emotional palate like a good sorbet between courses. The rhythm of these rides allows me to retrieve pieces of myself that have broken off and gotten lost over the previous year. As I rode my bike in the summer of 2015 it grew clear to me that it was time to fully open the door to my deepest wound already being forced open by the resonance with my teenage kids. Each inch they grew, each milestone that passed threw me headlong into my own frozen place, setting up a standoff within me. If I could not look at my life at seventeen, I would become that traumatized and disconnected mother—I would leave them emotionally, replaying for them a smaller version of my own world exploding at this age.

On a ride after a fresh rainstorm, with thick mud clogging my brakes and splattering the back of my shirt, I simply knew I needed to face, once and for all, my father's murder and Isaac's wrongful conviction. Not knowing whether this was another wild goose chase designed to avoid my pain or an honest attempt to heal, as my children turned seventeen, I consciously decided to take action. I shared this with no one.

My brooding shifted into a plan—I would search for Laurie White, the lawyer who had represented Isaac when he was finally released from prison, and ask if we could talk. That same night, as the light dimmed over the trees at the preserve, Jayme and Judy sat at the puzzle table, and Alex was at his computer, I Googled Laurie White and discovered she was now a judge in New Orleans. I sent a message to a non-specific address listed on her webpage.

Hello—my name is Dr. Amy Banks. I am a psychiatrist in Lexington, MA. Many years ago, Att. Laurie White was involved in successfully exonerating the alleged killer of my father, Dr. Ronald Banks. The young man accused of his murder was Isaac Knapper. I contacted her a number of years ago and she did get back to me, but I was not clear what information I needed. I am now hoping to have a conversation with her about the case. Wondering if she has any of the case files left—I do believe this all happened pre-Katrina. There is some interesting information that I have discovered about my father that may or may not help explain his murder and I am trying to find out if she has any more information about the real assailants, I can be reached at my email. I am hoping someone can get back to me about this…I am willing to travel to New Orleans to meet with her if that would be helpful. Thanks so much, Amy Banks.

When I pressed "send" on July 14, 2015 at 8:54 p.m., it felt like pressing hyperspace in the old Asteroids game. I had just launched myself somewhere but had no idea where I would pop up. I tried to trust that this would unfold as it should. I closed my computer and, with my heart racing, sat at the puzzle table for some distraction. Knowing the way government offices work, I assumed I might be in for a long wait. And so, when an email popped up in my account less than twenty-four hours later, directly from Judge Laurie White, I was stunned.

Dear Dr. Banks,

I just received your email. I would be glad to speak to you. I am not sure if I still have the case files as I purged most records when I became a judge eight years ago. Please feel free to email me at my address which this is being sent from. Laurie White

I wrote back that same day expressing my gratitude that she wrote so quickly and asking if we could schedule a time to talk by phone about Isaac's exoneration and any other information she might have discovered about my father's murder.

During the time since Isaac's conviction was overturned, curious questions arose about my father's possible involvement with the CIA in the late sixties and seventies. Apparently, during the Cold War there was a little-known program run by the U.S. that recruited history professors to spy on the Russians. The historians traveled to Eastern-bloc countries allegedly for academic study and while there, gathered intelligence information. In fact, in 1967 my father traveled to the Czech Republic and Prague with a group of university professors—an unusual trip given that my father's specialty was United States and Maine history. And then there was my family's move to Switzerland when I was in fourth grade. We were scheduled to live there for a year but fled after two months, allegedly because we did not have the housing that was promised us. As my siblings and I grasped for straws about what might have happened to our father if Isaac was not the killer, we began to consider something more sinister. This was encouraged by Phil's late-night emails which frequently referenced our father's role in the CIA. At one point, Phil sent me an itinerary issued to my father for an orientation visit to Offutt Air Force Base (at the time, the site of the United States Strategic Air Command) just before going to the Czech Republic. While this information all seemed intriguing, in retrospect it was far-fetched to think my father had been involved in a larger conspiracy, as so many strange, improbable things had already happened in our lives.

From the first time we made contact, Laurie's return emails were open and generous. In her second email she suggested a time to talk the following Monday, admitting her memory for details might not be the best after over twenty years since Isaac's exoneration. Even with a plan to speak in place, we still shared emails back and forth—she seemed curious that I was reaching out after all this time and also a little surprised that I was not angry with her for having gotten Isaac exonerated. In one exchange I shared the following reflection:

> I am appreciative of anything you can offer re: the case. I was just Isaac Knapper's age (sixteen-seventeen) when my father was murdered, my brother went to the trial and I will never forget the description he gave of the grief Isaac Knapper's family had when the decision was read. Certainly, many lives were ruined over this.

Laurie's response was warm, and she seemed genuinely interested in hearing about our family.

> Amy
> Please call me Laurie.
> I'm afraid I have no recollection of you and me ever talking before…perhaps I was so shocked that I lost the memory…. I would probably have been expecting you were going to be a very angry person at me for getting him released from the charge. Was I helpful or what were the circumstances of our prior interaction?
>
> I find it interesting that you are a psychiatrist. It would seem understandable to go into that field due to such a great loss of a parent and you were so young. But of course that may not have had anything to do with your career choice. How long have you been a psychiatrist? What do you do?

What do you know about Isaac or the case...that I may have told you or you have learned on your own? What is your main reason to reach out to me? Not that you have to have a reason. I'm just curious. Did your mother remarry? How was your family affected? How were you and each of your siblings affected...you said your brother was at the trial and remembered Isaac's family's grief. It could not have compared to your brother's grief. Theirs was just fresher."
LAW

In my follow-up email, I tried to address some of the questions she asked and also provided her with an overview of my family and the impact the murder had on each of us. I was starving for information and felt a palpable relief to be communicating with someone who had intimate knowledge of what had happened to my family and to Isaac. While I was not entirely sure what I was looking for in a conversation, I did share that she and I had not talked when I reached out to her, as I was not ready, and I also recounted what we had been able to discover about Isaac's release and subsequent life and return to prison. I was able to organize two questions in my mind that related to her work with Isaac. First: did she find any other irregularities in the case that might lead her to believe my father's murder was part of a larger government conspiracy? And secondly, how and why was she convinced that Isaac did not do the killing?

Laurie's email back was filled with information that felt like a salve to the wound. She was funny and clear. As I read her words, I could feel the very deep and tight emotional knot begin to loosen.

Wow....lots there. Thank you for the information about your family.

I am so glad to learn about Dr. Banks's family even if it all is not happy. Your family was so affected by the crime and that crime had such far-reaching effects on so many people that the victimization is always so extensive. Such loss.

I was a prosecutor for the Orleans DA's office and after I left to join an insurance defense firm, a lawyer reached out to me when Isaac's mother was looking for a lawyer to represent Isaac at a hearing granted by the LA SP [supreme] court. The hearing was granted as a result of a jail house legal filing. The judge for that hearing was Frank Shea who had also been the judge at trial. Judge Shea hated most lawyers and especially every woman lawyer...except me. I had been a prosecutor in his section and, in fact, the first woman he allowed to be in his section of court for longer than one day. On about the third day in his court, I asked him why he had been on the bench for twenty-five years and not allowed women to practice in his court and why was he allowing me to stay and not throw me out...like he did the others. He told me, "'Cause you got a fine ass and a dirty mouth!" I asked him how he knew about either of those! He looked like an unhappy George Burns and was a salty old bastard. He never did anyone a favor...including me nor Isaac. But I loved the old Koot! He mentored me, rather unusually, but it was the only type of mentoring I got in the "women in courtroom" setting of the 1980s.

Anyway, Isaac was my first criminal client and I took the case because I knew that prosecutors did not, and would not, cheat. I wanted to see for myself because I knew I would be thorough in my investigation, review, and representation and would find that a prosecutor had not cheated. Well, needless to say, I was stunned to find that the prosecutor and police officer had withheld such important information. The case shaped my entire legal career and my ideas still to this day about integrity and ethics in law.

Ultimately, Judge Shea denied Isaac any relief and the case progressed on writs to the LA Supreme Court. Isaac's conviction was ultimately reversed by that court and by that time I was a sex crimes prosecutor in Baton Rouge. Isaac was released eventually. I was planning to file a civil suit and expected we would all be rich for the malicious prosecution civil damages he would receive. Well, that did not happen, but many more interesting things did.

I made my fiancé babysit Isaac so he wouldn't get into any trouble while I was getting the civil suit going. I was still in Baton Rouge as a prosecutor. My fiancé (husband now—twenty-two years) was in NOLA [New Orleans, Louisiana] and became a pal with him since I asked him to watch him (Isaac). Well, Isaac asked Tom to work with him in boxing, to protect him in that world of boxing...and Tom began joining him at the local boxing gym to watch and learn and be involved.

I moved back to NOLA and we ultimately became the owners and managers of this inner-city boxing gym. We helped lots of kids but Isaac was very special. He was like a boy raised by wolves from his time in prison, yet he was so amazingly immature, naïve, and he lacked hatred or resentment towards anyone for his situation; yet, he had killer instincts in the boxing ring, with more heart than anyone I had ever known (boxing had served him well and saved him in prison). He went on to be a Golden Gloves champ and competed nationally to be on the U.S. boxing team.

After that great hope was dashed, then the civil suit fell apart. As a result of the civil suit...the ruling was that all Louisiana prosecutors received absolute immunity from civil damages, thus it was okay that he had been convicted by cheating prosecutors. I went on to file an attorney disciplinary charge against the prosecutor twenty years later for his actions in not turning over the report. These were the first formal charges ever accepted against a prosecutor for such actions.

Isaac's life didn't seem to have any kind of bright future by this time and now he had a wife and children. He worked at different menial jobs but there was nothing he really could do; he did not have his GED or any trade. He didn't know how to work or do anything and only knew ex-cons from jail.

He became a professional boxer and my husband and I managed and promoted his professional boxing career. He went all over the world boxing. We spent a bunch of money on the gym and kids and Isaac, till we finally threw in the towel after he broke his hand. We all came to the realization that boxing was not going to be his ticket either.

He got hooked up with a white kid that had boxed with him in another gym and started moving drugs for that kid's drug source from Mexico. The white kid died from a drug overdose and Isaac moved into a bigger role with the drug-moving, as it was profitable.

He lost his freedom again, this time for being a drug dealer. He managed to involve his whole family: wife, girl-friend, cousins, and friends in a federal conspiracy. I was his lawyer initially but not after the feds threatened him by telling him that they were going to involve me in the conspiracy. Isaac removed me as his lawyer. My husband and I both tried to explain to him that they could not hurt me because I was NOT involved in the drugs or anything illegal and that it was just a scare tactic they were using on him.

Isaac could not trust that the government would not do to me like he had been done to before and that I would get railroaded and harmed. He ended up with a "less invested" attorney and entered a plea that I never would have let him agree to. The whole group in the conspiracy charge all pled guilty and Isaac received the longest sentence of twenty-two+ years. I cried every time I heard from him for the first ten years of his sentence…my sadness was based on so much lost.

Isaac has never drunk, smoked, or used drugs. He has his GED now. Isaac has one son, Isaac Jr., who turned twenty-two years old this July. Isaac Jr. has a younger sister, Isis, sixteen years old now. These are Isaac's kids from his marriage to Nicki. They are divorced now but still very close and communicate. Nicki moved the kids to the

Houston area after Katrina and they are all doing great. Isaac has daughters with 2 (or 3) other women also. He is crazy about all his kids. He has great relationships with all his kids and talks to them almost daily. He has been a very involved father even from prison.

I always heard that there was a big lawsuit against the Hyatt for their lack of security, and your family was represented by Ralph Whalen, a local attorney, and that he got your family a large, undisclosed amount of money as a settlement (I hope that was the case). I heard that the prosecutor, Dave Paddison was also involved in the civil lawsuit in some way. Any truth to that?

The case should have been re-opened or declared an unsolved murder by the NOPD or at the insistence of the prosecutor but sadly that was not done that I know of.

I decided with this very first criminal client not to make a decision on a client's guilt or innocence. I handled each case as a legal technician—applying the law to the facts. I was never a lawyer that professed any client's innocence (except a client that was exonerated from DNA that proved scientifically that he was not the rapist). I always had opinions about a client's guilt and the prosecutor in me basically always thought all clients had committed the crime accused of until I proved it otherwise to myself and based on the facts of the case and my investigation.

I don't believe that Isaac killed your father. The facts did not show him to be the perpetrator and what I know of him and what I have learned from him I do not think or believe that he was even there on the night of the crime.

As I read Laurie's email, I could feel something deep inside of me shift. The description of Isaac as naïve, immature, an involved father to his children, a big heart, a boy raised by wolves in prison kept running through my mind.

I wrote back:

Hi Laurie—a WOW back to you for all of this information.

I am so sorry to hear the circumstances of Isaac's return to jail—how much longer does he have to serve? Clearly he has become much more than a legal client to you and your husband. You asked about a lawsuit—a lawyer by the name of Stephen Murray reached out to our family and suggested we could file a lawsuit against the Hyatt Regency—that there had been many burglaries in that area and the hotel should have warned its guests (like they did their own employees) that it was not safe to walk around there after dark. We won the case—the reward did not make us wealthy— the original lawsuit was for many millions of dollars. We ended up with a reward that reflected the wages lost from my father's future employment and some for emotional damage—it ended up being around $975,000. Certainly, it allowed my mother to not have to worry about money for the time she was alive—but the lawsuit was also appealed by the Hyatt all the way to the Louisiana Supreme Court and that took many years and, unfortunately, kept the murder alive. The case is now a landmark case in hotel security (*Banks vs Hyatt*) and I do feel quite good about that. I do not recognize the name, Ralph Whalen—though maybe he was working with Steve Murray—but Dave Paddison is familiar, though I couldn't say from what trials. I was still pretty young when all of this was going on and for most of it I was away at either college or medical school so would get the information secondhand.

However, as you may be able to imagine, I still would like to know the circumstances of the murder—particularly whether it was a hold-up by someone other than Isaac and Leroy Williams or was it bigger than that? From what you have written, I feel more comfortable that Isaac was not the one who shot my father, and, in fact, I feel terrible that he got dragged into something that clearly has changed the course of his life as well as the life of his family—what a sense of powerlessness they all must feel against this corrupt system.

We wrote back and forth over the next few days trying to find a time to talk on the phone. After so much anxious anticipation, I was amazed at how easy it was to walk through this door and how relieving.

After the first few emails, I had shared with my partner the exchanges I was having with Laurie. Jayme and Alex were sixteen years old, and though not directly involved in the conversation, were listening in around the edges. When Jayme joined me on a bike ride around the lake one afternoon, I took the opportunity to ask how she was doing with this information and her response was powerful. She said it was devastating to hear. However, the "it" to which she referred was not clear to me and so I asked what she meant by that. She wasn't focused on the murder, the death of her grandfather, the open murder case and what that might be like for our family. She zeroed in immediately on where the weight of the injustice lay—she couldn't believe that a young man had been locked up all that time for a crime he had not committed.

When Laurie and I finally talked a few days later, she shared that Isaac had recently been released from federal prison after serving seventeen years of his federal sentence for selling drugs. In that moment I knew I would meet him. My reaching out at the exact same time he had been released from prison felt like far more than a lucky coincidence; it felt like fate. I recognized that standing face-to-face with Isaac had been a longing from the first day I saw him in that grainy newspaper clipping in 1979. I was drawn to him in a way I was not to his alleged accomplice, Leroy Williams. At the time I thought I simply needed to see the man, the boy who had pulled the trigger and killed my father. I needed him to help me understand why he did it. What forces in his life conspired so that he was in front of the Hyatt Regency with a gun at the exact moment my father was returning from dinner. It wasn't that I thought he would simply tell me these things, but I carried some vague notion that if I looked into his eyes and heard his voice, the confusion of what had happened to my life would magically clear.

In our first conversation, as Laurie and I were sharing incredible facts of this shared story, she mentioned that I needed to write a book about this, that it was a story that needed to be told. I deflected the statement back to her saying she needed to write the book, but when she explained she could not because she was a judge, I paused. I had just finished a book project I had been working on for five years and was actually trying to think about my next writing project. Laurie planted a seed, and as I continued my rides through the PLP preserve, the seed blossomed. By the time my family and I left the PLP to return to Lexington, it was crystal clear to me that I did need to write about this; nothing was more important than telling this story.

Laurie and I continued our conversation by email over the next few weeks and she eventually sent me a recent photo of her and Isaac, warning me that he was a big guy who might look frightening. I couldn't stop looking at the picture that captured their closeness, intimacy, and honest affection. He was no longer the boy in those newspaper clippings; his face was now widened with age, his body built up from working out. He wore a yellow V-neck Lacoste T-shirt over a tank top. His eyes were gentle and in one photo I imagined fatigue, but all things considered, Isaac looked surprisingly robust given the twenty-nine years he had spent in prison.

After returning home from the PLP in late July, Judy, Alex, and I were sitting on the couch in the living room, and I decided to show them the pictures of Isaac and Laurie. I wanted to know what they saw—does he look menacing or scary or even murderous? They agreed that he did not, but then Alex asked the question that lingers in the background of my consciousness: "What if he did do it?" And that question catches the deep neurological groove I have spent thirty-six years feeding—the pathway that connects Isaac Knapper to the murder of my father.

Isaac had already been freed, absolved of the crime by the State of Louisiana. But what did I need to do to absolve him from the death, to erase or starve that neural pathway that tied any mention of Isaac or Knapper to the horrific night of April 12, 1979. And why did it matter? Because it was always there, traumatic images ready to intrude and disrupt even the most basic or happiest days of my life. A relative named Isaac comes for Thanksgiving and I am fighting off memories of that night each time someone calls his name. My partner says she is taking a nap; there he is again, hands cuffed behind his back, an angry scowl on his face, pulling me into that deep, traumatic memory. It lives at the core of who I am, bubbling in my guts, squishing my lungs, choking me. The association can come so fast at times—rap, cap, nap, Knapper, father, murder, death. I run fast and furiously away; it will not get me, cannot get me, but it is always nipping at my heels ready to swallow me whole if only I stop. I do not stop. It becomes clear that breaking this connection, absolving, exonerating Isaac from my father's death will require stopping and looking into the eyes of the beast. To risk being swallowed whole. The beast is not Knapper; the beast is the terror and the grief, the fear that if I start crying I simply may never stop.

And so I sat in front of my computer, poised to write a letter to Isaac Knapper, who had been in my life for so, so many years, with full awareness that I was pushing the door to my deepest pain wide open.

21

FINDING ISAAC

Amy Banks

What do I write to the man wrongly convicted of murdering my father? Should I address the letter to Isaac, the young teen sent to prison, or to the grown man, Mr. Knapper, as an honest sign of respect for all he has survived? Should I mention the murder or his wrongful conviction, or keep it simple and just ask for a meeting? As I sat staring at my computer screen, I realized that the intimacy of our shared circumstances makes me feel like I've known him forever, but actually, I know nothing about him. My ignorance is crystal clear as I compose an invitation to meet.

August 15, 2015
Dear Mr. Knapper,

Let me start by introducing myself. My name is Amy Banks and I am the daughter of Ronald Banks. It is with much anxiety that I write to you today to introduce myself and to ask to meet you. There are a couple of things that I want to say up front by way of reassurance. First, while my father's murder was an overwhelming tragedy to my family and those who loved him, it was made a billion times worse when we discovered that you had been wrongly convicted due to police misconduct. Of course I could never know what those years were like for you and your family while you were a young man in Angola. But I do try. I have a seventeen-year-old son, and I literally feel sick thinking of him in that situation. All of you must have suffered so deeply. I will be forever grateful that Laurie White believed in you and in justice.

The second thing I would like you to know is that my family has no interest at this point in reopening the case. I simply would like to know what you know about the murder. I have wanted to meet you from the first time I heard your name. Part of it may have been that we are the same age, but even when I thought you had been the shooter, I still could not feel anger. Not sure what that was about

At this stage in my life, I am a psychiatrist and deeply committed to social justice and particularly the ongoing racism that continues to foster systems of corruption, like the one that existed in New Orleans thirty-five years ago that framed you for a murder you did not commit. With those things in mind, I would love to meet with you in whatever setting and with whomever you would like near you. My younger sister, Nancy, would come with me. She was eight when my father was killed and has a very similar commitment to justice. If you are open to this, we would figure out a time to come to New Orleans that works for you. Hope to hear back from you and again, thank you for reading this.

With deep respect,
Amy Banks

On August 12, 2015—thirteen thousand two hundred and seventy-one days after our lives grotesquely collided—I pushed the send button on my Gmail account and transmitted the letter to Laurie White, who had promised to pass it along to Isaac. She had already told him that I had been in touch, and she said he was open to some contact, but even with that reassurance I had to wonder, what I was doing. One week passed, and then two, and I heard nothing back. My mind was spinning. Maybe I said too much, maybe I said too little. Maybe he thinks I'm a white asshole. Maybe Laurie went on vacation and doesn't check her email. Maybe I *am* a white asshole. Maybe Isaac is trying to settle his life after seventeen years in prison and my life and my healing is not at the top of his priority list. Maybe he won't respond and will have changed his mind about meeting. Maybe I should have left this whole mess alone.

Finally, a response came: He'd meet with me if it would help. His response could have been to run for the hills, to want no reminders of the event that robbed him of twelve years of his life, but instead, he was willing to meet "if it would help." This was our first real interaction after decades of meetings in my mind, and I was moved by its simplicity and generosity.

How in the world do our paths cross, a seventeen-year-old white girl from Brewer, Maine, and a seventeen-year-old Black boy from New Orleans? Everything tangible told me that we would never meet, but I became connected to Isaac under the worst circumstances imaginable and he was now knitted into my very being, even though I'd never met him. This man—who was sustained by a mother who never gave up on his innocence and a girlfriend who supported him through his second imprisonment—who had spent twenty-nine years in prison, was willing to meet me "if it would help." I was driven by a curiosity to meet him, to know him, to express my outrage at his wrongful incarceration and my grief at how my father's murder robbed him of his youth. Despite my medical and psychiatric training, I struggled to understand the intensity of my desire to meet this man. What could possibly explain it? Perhaps it is simply human connection—the thing I have been thinking and writing about for decades now. As humans, we are capable of unimaginable violence and deep kindnesses, as well as the capacity to feel one another, and in that feeling we are enlarged and improved, even in the deepest pain. In feeling another person, we are invited to become whole. Maybe in some cosmic, karmic way, a connection with Isaac would buffer the agony of losing the primal connection with my father.

And I desperately wanted to be whole again, even if the process killed me. Sending the letter to Isaac had opened the floodgates in my soul, and I became ravenous for information about my father and that night. He has been crystallized as a two-dimensional tragic figure in my mind since the day of his murder. As I reached out to Isaac, I began to realize the future I had lost the night my father was shot. Who was this man I had called Dad for seventeen years? I felt a frantic need to fill in the many blanks, so I decided to call his best friend, Charlie.

A few weeks later, as I drove the two hours to Cape Elizabeth, I played the phone conversation with Charlie over and over in my mind. I had not talked with him since my mother's funeral seventeen years earlier, but his response to hearing my voice was classic: "Holy smokes," spoken with a deep warmth that easily transmitted his pleasure at hearing from me. Charlie leaves very few spaces for insecurity in a relationship. He is at once warm, sincere, and very funny. An olive-skinned Greek American man who looked, at age eighty-six, much as he had at age forty-six. His thick, black hair was now shorter and white, his face wizened but not wrinkled, his posture that of a twenty-six-year-old athlete, straight and steady. He still runs five miles a day on the same bowlegs he had in his youth. When we talked on the phone, he said matter-of-factly, "Your father was the best friend I ever had." He spoke of the times they shared as young academics at the University of Maine in Orono—every story ending with the two of them doubled over in laughter, tears rolling down their faces. He clearly enjoyed the contrast of two serious academics laughing with abandon as though they were children at a park, not colleagues in a serious meeting. Although I never saw this wildly funny side of my father, I do remember the background noise of my father's witty one-liners that I hadn't been old enough to appreciate.

When I shifted gears and asked Charlie about the night of the murder, his eyes grew a little more distant and a brief look of confusion and fatigue swept over his face. His sentences were broken and his voice filled with emotion of some sort—it was hard to pin it down. His eyes were moist with tears that never overflowed onto his cheeks. I recognized this as a traumatic grief response, one that offered no real release from the pain. He reminded me that Bob Babcock, the chair of the history department, had heard the news, maybe from Judy Hakola, and drove the twenty minutes from Orono to Brewer to break the news to my mother. Somehow they both pulled into the driveway within seconds of each other, and Charlie was relieved that Bob had told my mother about my father's death so he didn't have to. As I tried to imagine this scene, which took place just moments before all hell broke loose in my house, my heart broke for this gentle soul faced with the agonizing task of sharing the news of his best friend's murder with his now-widowed wife, a woman he had grown to love dearly through the years. How fortunate that he was ultimately a witness rather than the messenger. According to Charlie's account, my mother simply refused to believe it, while my brother woke, heard the news, and simply said, "Jesus Christ."

As I drove back to Lexington, a holographic image of Charlie and my father floated in my mind. My dad, at six foot four, towered over Charlie's five-and-a-half-foot frame. They were the Mutt and Jeff of academia, with the energy of two mischievous teenage boys enjoying the antics of the other. I remembered the stories I heard growing up of the two of them at a department store or library, paging another friend overhead simply to embarrass him. My dad and Charlie would stand off to the side, giggling, as their friend or colleague walked to the front desk bewildered. And suddenly images of that playful dad popped into my mind. I could see him crawling on the floor with Nancy on his back when she was a toddler, and I remembered the times that I would tell him he was growing a belly and he would immediately drop to the ground, complete a set of sit-ups, and then pop back up, sucking in his gut and showing off his suddenly slim physique. As these images ran through my mind, the pain in my heart, the ache and the longing, was excruciating. Only in that moment did I realize how protective the deep freeze had been, but also how it had robbed me of the deep grief that is emotionally and physiologically needed to survive the loss of a parent. For thirty-five years the experience of losing my father has been dominated by his murder: the raw, blood and guts of violence, hijacked by legal arguments and lawsuits. And now, finally, there was a soft spot in me where a child sat, knees drawn to her chest, weeping, scared, and alone with the knowledge that her daddy was gone forever.

After I met with Charlie, I reached out to others who were a part of that night. I called John Hakola's wife, Judy, and my old basketball coach, Linda Clohosey, who was the first person I had reached out to after hearing about the murder.

Judy was still living in the home she shared with John on the edge of the University of Maine campus, so I wrote a letter and snail-mailed it. I wasn't sure if it would actually reach her, and I was even less sure that she'd respond to my request to talk about that night. Would she be willing to open this old wound, which must have changed the course of her life just as clearly as it had my own?

Weeks went by with no answer, so I reached out to Charlie, who gave me her email address. I was greatly relieved when she returned my message right away, and a few days later we spoke on the phone.

Judy's voice was peppy and upbeat, offering little evidence of the wear and tear inflicted by seventy-five years of life. The conversation felt easy, as though we were long-lost friends who had simply been distracted by our own kids and careers. She told me that after John suffered a massive stroke that left him unable to talk, she returned to work to support their three young children. She was still working as a professor, teaching English to engineering students at the university where her husband and my dad had both worked.

She told me that John had never spoken about that night, had never shared the rush of terror he experienced as he looked at the masked faces and the chrome gun, or the absolute helplessness he felt as he witnessed his good friend die on the pavement in front of him. I assumed his silence was evidence of an extreme, traumatic-freeze reaction, but Judy quickly set me straight: "John did not talk about anything—ever," she said. "At least not about his feelings."

Despite his silence, she could feel the wound in his behavior and demeanor, saying that "he was simply shattered." She told me that John had been in charge of grad students at the university in the early to late 60s, when my father was pursuing his PhD, and John had immediately liked him. In fact, my father had been one of his first graduate students, and Judy was quite sure that John had been my father's dissertation advisor. I had no idea how intimately John had nurtured my father's intellect, and it allowed me to fill in some gaping holes about my dad with imagined conversations and debates that the two of them must have had through the years as my father grew from a student to an admired colleague. John had lost so much in New Orleans.

On the night of the murder, John called Judy at around ten o'clock, some forty-five minutes after the shooting, to tell her that my mother must be told. He asked her to contact my parents' best friends, Charlie and Joanne, and to instruct them to get to my mother as soon as possible. That drive, twenty minutes from Orono to Brewer, was surely the stuff of nightmares, as Charlie and Joanne braced themselves to deliver the devastating news. John wasn't free to come home, to return to the only place that could hold a modicum of safety. He would be stuck in New Orleans for the next few days playing out the murder over and over again for the detectives. He returned home with my father's body five days later. Members of the history department—dressed in suits and ties, casual sweaters, and somber, shocked faces—greeted both.

Judy told me that John's working life ended just two years later, when he was barely fifty. We'll never know if the murder of his friend caused the massive stroke that devastated his body, especially since John was one of fifteen children who had each developed early heart problems. He'd had his first heart attack at age forty-one, long before his trip to New Orleans. But he had rehabbed and was back hiking Mount Katahdin and other tall peaks in northern Maine. It's likely that his massive stroke was simply a perfect storm of genetics and stress.

Judy was clear that he was heavily burdened by survivor guilt when he returned to Maine. As the history department worked to cover my father's grad students and classes for the rest of the year, John signed up for all of them. He felt it was his obligation. His workload increased dangerously, and he became even more distant than usual, with no real way to express the turmoil that was eating away at him. Judy remembered one poignant afternoon when a neighbor watched their kids for the day, giving them some much-needed time alone. They drove down east (in Maine parlance, that means "toward the coast") to wander through the local potter's shops, and at one point they stopped at Schoodic Point, where John sat quietly on the rocks and stared silently over the vast ocean. He was miles and miles away.

Within a year he was back in New Orleans, testifying at the criminal trial. Judy knew that he dreaded the trip, but he was determined to fulfill what he felt was his obligation to the case and to my father. When he was asked on the stand to identify the killer, he couldn't. Not only had his glasses been knocked off when he was pushed into the door during the assault, but the assailants had worn masks. As he sat on the witness stand, he must have relived the helplessness of the night, unable to provide the testimony that would unequivocally bring justice to his friend's death but honest enough to say only what he could recall.

The trial must have added another layer of guilt and trauma to his psyche. As the stress increased, his heart disease progressed. The following year he underwent quadruple bypass surgery, and just three weeks after the surgery he suffered a massive stroke that left him unable to express any complex inner thoughts. He was able to write a lecture for students but couldn't process a conceptual question they might ask about the material. At home, Judy described him as moody and dysregulated, throwing tantrums like a two-year-old and barely able to help her with the tasks around the house or parent his children. He was trapped in this prison for the remaining eleven years of his life. The Hakola family became part of the extensive collateral damage unleashed that night.

When I emailed Linda Clohosey, my former coach, she returned the message right away and agreed to meet for lunch. At the restaurant, I asked her about that night, what she remembered, what it was like. Linda had always had a flair for the dramatic, and I remembered this when she immediately compared it to the impact of hearing about the Kennedy assassination. With great clarity, she stated that she would never forget the moment she heard about my father's murder. She was in her apartment about to go to sleep when she answered my call and knew immediately that something was terribly wrong by the tone of my voice—barely a whisper, as she remembered it—as I blurted out that something bad had happened and my father was dead. She rushed to our house and stayed throughout the evening, a witness to my mother's collapse and a houseful of frozen, grief-stricken faces. She told me that my mother seemed to move in and out of acceptance of the news, and that she had never seen anyone as devastated. Her recollections resonated with the horror I remember from that evening. In fact, every person I've talked to who was there that night has confirmed my worst fears of just how bad it really was.

The re-creation of an event like that from a number of people's broken, traumatized recollections is like putting together a puzzle without having an image of the final product as a guide. People move in and out of focus, depending on who is sharing the story and what role they played in trying to help my family cope with the tragic news. I've begun to realize that I'll never have a truly complete, coherent account of that night—I might put the pieces together, but there will always be missing data, sheared from the memory of those who were there by time and trauma.

Communication between Isaac and me was facilitated by Laurie White, and coordinating the schedules of four people in three far-flung cities wasn't easy. But we finally settled on the weekend of December 14, 2015, when Nancy and I would fly from New York to New Orleans. At one point during my conversations with Laurie, she told me about the prison-reform program that she and a colleague had started at Angola, and she invited us to visit. We readily accepted, unaware at that time that Isaac and his wife would be joining us.

I then contacted David Paddison, the lawyer who prosecuted Isaac for the murder, to ask if he would meet with Nancy and me. He responded through his secretary that he would be happy to help us in any way he could, and just days before we were scheduled to fly to New Orleans, he left a message asking me to call him. Hearing his Southern drawl made the trip a little more real, the knot in my stomach a little tighter. When I called him back he was warm and gracious and asked about my family. He also reaffirmed his certainty about the guilty verdict, adding almost incredulously that "they came after me," a reference to Laurie and Isaac's pursuit of disciplinary action against him for withholding evidence at the trial.

During our phone conversation he mentioned that he still had a large box of documents from the original and appeals trials that he would gladly share with us. In fact, he offered to tell us the "whole, great story," if we were "up to hearing it." It was only after that conversation that I began to wonder what he meant by that last part—I couldn't help imagining that in this large box of facts and papers about my father's death there was a picture of the crime scene, my father lying dead on the sidewalk, blood pooled around the back of his head, his brown tie bunched over his chest and still clipped to his shirt. I both wanted and needed to see it, but I felt repulsed by the image I'd created. I'd already unearthed one photo from the April 14, 1979, edition of the *Times-Picayune*, an image that hit me like a sucker punch and took my breath away. My father's long, dead body is lying on the street covered by a white sheet, while the Reverend Peter Rogers stands over him and administers the last rites. It's an intimate moment watched over by a cadre of police officers and detectives, notepads in hand, grim faces witnessing the death of another man on the streets of New Orleans.

Paddison graciously offered to bring the box of documents to our hotel; he suggested that we find a private conference room for a few hours so he could share his story. In our earlier email exchange, I had mentioned that I was planning to write a book about my father's murder, and for the first time I started to suspect that he wanted to get his side of the story into print. He proudly shared that he had tried more than thirty murder cases in his career, and that nine of those men were on death row. In fact, in one case the man he put to death already had a book written about him.

When we hung up the phone I felt a surprising lack of guilt about not telling him Nancy and I were planning to meet Isaac before we sat down with him, that I believed in Isaac's innocence, and that I was appalled at the outcome of the case. I wanted to tell him that putting an innocent boy in jail did not serve my family well, that it hurt us even more, and that it marred my father's memory and further complicated the complex grief that had been frozen for years in my body. I thought I might say these things to him in person, but I wasn't really sure.

A week before we were scheduled to travel to New Orleans, Laurie sent me an email reporting that she had lost contact with Isaac. Though she said it without a hint of concern, I immediately imagined the worst—that he'd been injured or even killed—and I was surprised at how deeply fearful and anxious I was. I also realized that I had no idea what his actual day-to-day life was like—whom he saw, the contacts he was making. How in the world was he adapting to life out of prison for the first time in seventeen years? In my small, self-interested world, it was unnerving to contemplate traveling all the way to New Orleans only to have him not show up. Laurie assured me that it would still work out, that Isaac might be mad at her, so she gave me the phone number of Isaac's mother, Clara, who could always reach him. A couple of days before we were scheduled to travel, I tentatively called Clara, filled with an awareness of the injustice her family had been through.

Although our conversation was relatively brief, the impact it had on me was profound. I nervously introduced myself and told her how sorry I was for the wrongful conviction of her son. She accepted my words with kindness and shared that one of her daughters, one of Isaac's sisters, had just passed away in the last couple of weeks. My heart broke for this mother who had suffered unfathomable losses over the years.

When I asked her about the night of the murder, her honesty and integrity simply took my breath away. "They wanted me to testify that Isaac was in the house that night," she told me, "but like most nights, there was so much going on. The boys were in and out like they were most nights." She couldn't testify under oath that he was in the house the entire night of the murder because she wasn't sure. She told me she couldn't lie, even to save her son's life. I would later learn that Isaac wasn't able to lie under oath and say that Leroy Williams killed my father, even though it might have saved him from a life conviction. When we hung up the phone I sat quietly and tried to digest her words, unsure of how to understand the strength, dignity, and decency I had just witnessed.

22

THREATENED

Isaac Knapper

After spending almost thirty years in prison, life is now pretty good. I am working for the park system for the City of New Orleans doing maintenance work. The 250 parks in New Orleans were a wonderful surprise to me. After work I routinely go to the gym to work out and to train young boxers. One big surprise is that I am now training young women boxers and they are terrific!

For any ex-inmate the transition back to the free world is difficult. For me the biggest challenges have been simply starting over in my life in my mid-fifties. I've had to adjust to being comfortable around other people. This requires me to shed the hypervigilance necessary in prison to stay alive. Many of the challenges have been emotional. By far my biggest challenge has been overcoming my sadness and regret about missing so much of my children's lives. I missed those early years when they needed a father to hug and hold them. I feel blessed that my daughter Ivory gave birth to her first son and my first grandson, Noah, last year. They live with Denise and me now, which means I am getting a second chance at raising a child.

When I share my story with folks now, I am often asked how I survived all these years and the answer is crystal clear to me. I am a fighter. I mean that literally in that building a reputation as an accomplished boxer allowed me to establish a reputation that few men wanted to challenge, but being a boxer also gave me the mental strength to deal with most anything the prison system threw at me, from physical assaults to purposelessly humiliating and demoralizing actions from guards and correctional officers. One clear goal I had was to maintain my dignity throughout my incarceration. I had learned this from my mother and it has served me well through these many, long years.

By far the biggest surprise since leaving prison was when Dr. Banks's daughter reached out to me. When Laurie called to tell me that Dr. Banks's daughters were trying to meet me, I was skeptical. The request was completely out of the blue—a little shocking and very worrisome. My initial thought was, *Oh, here it goes again; it's all going to be opened back up.* I had recently been transferred from the Pollack Camp to the halfway house for the remaining few months of my sentence. I was closer to home in New Orleans than I had been in a decade and a half, and I was focused on my future and building a life after all I had lost. Denise and I were planning our wedding in a few weeks and were ready to put my imprisonment behind us. Finally I would have the time and space to build real adult relationships with my children. To do the simple things in life—to work, to box, to love freely. Denise was even more skeptical and scared than I was. She was worried that somehow I could be placed in another situation where I was charged or in trouble. She had waited seventeen years to have me home and meeting with these women was not only a major distraction but took us back to the most difficult part of our lives. She felt protective of me and wanted to know what they wanted with me.

But still, there was a small part of me that thought, *If they want it, I'll do it.* In part this came from a sense of connection I always felt with the younger daughter, Nancy. I remember clearly sitting in my cell in the Parish Prison and then in Angola and thinking about Dr. Banks's younger daughter, who was only eight years old when he was killed. I wanted to reach out and to comfort her in any way I could back then, but, of course, I was also sure they would not want to hear from me. I guess a part of me was still curious to find out what they wanted.

23

MEETING

Amy Banks and Isaac Knapper

Amy –
The Omni Royal Orleans was our home away from home, our safe zone in New Orleans. Minutes after checking into the hotel and leaving our bags in the room, Nancy and I hiked to the Hyatt Regency. We hadn't discussed it ahead of time, but both of us instinctively knew that we needed to start this journey at the spot where our father took his last breath.

We exited the hotel in the French Quarter on a mission, passing dozens of people dressed for SantaCon, drunk and happy as they paraded down Bourbon Street. One woman was topless, her breasts painted red as she strolled passed the Hustler bar. We were so out of sync, detectives at a masquerade ball.

As we approached the Hyatt, it was hard to get oriented—so much had changed. The doorway where the murder had happened was gone; in fact, construction was underway at that very spot and the area cordoned off with a wire fence, men with hard hats actively working at the building site. The change was jarring. In my mind, that spot was a shrine, a sacred, immutable space, a place I could return to over and over again to honor my family's loss. I had imagined setting down a single rose, a simple marker of a life taken. But it had all been bulldozed. Later that weekend I learned that the entire hotel had been decimated in 2005 by Hurricane Katrina. The building and surrounding area was basically lifeless for six years before a major renovation project resuscitated it. The new and improved Hyatt was bigger, stronger, and even more grand than it had been back in 1979. The Hyatt had survived, but the shrine to my father was destroyed, accentuating the sense that his death was insignificant in the bigger scheme of things and that my family's pain didn't matter.

As we wandered through the Hyatt, it was easy to imagine the safety my father must have felt as he left that grand, opulent space, as though he had been tethered to the power and invulnerability of the building itself. I'm sure that being robbed never entered his mind. He was free to walk the streets, to chat with his colleague, to take in the unruly crowds and to return to the comfort of his hotel room for a good night's sleep before the conference started the following morning. He was so close—just four feet, forty-eight inches from true safety—when he was assaulted. His response—"You've got to be kidding"—was exactly his experience. Is this a joke; maybe a prank by one of his colleagues? Before he could make sense of the lethal danger he was in, a bullet had pierced his left eye. I suspect he died having no idea of the seriousness of the threat.

Nancy and I walked briskly back to the hotel as the sun was fading, fearful of being caught on the streets of New Orleans after dark. We passed the now drunker and more unruly crowds and settled into dinner with a bottle of Prosecco. Eating helped, drinking helped a little more.

Emotional eating is in our genes. My mother routinely made two desserts a day along with a full breakfast and dinner. There was almost no pain that couldn't be handled by her Hello Dollies or rich chocolate cake. Nancy and I ate our way through the four days in New Orleans. The first night following our trip to the Hyatt, I devoured filet mignon and buttered mashed potatoes, then ended the meal with two profiteroles—rich and creamy, and each shaped like a swan. The next day we would meet Isaac and Laurie.

On Sunday morning, Nancy and I walked the two miles to the courthouse from the posh French Quarter, through the medical center—with its soaring, pristine buildings—and eventually into the area around the courts, where most of the homes are small and run-down. We made an important pit stop along the way, stopping for a fortifying brunch at the Ruby Slipper on

Canal Street. We had planned to meet Laurie and Isaac in the early afternoon, but we ended up arriving ahead of time. It was Sunday; the courthouse was desolate, the surrounding bail-bond offices locked up tight, although the area would spring to life at eight the next morning as the weekend arrests were processed. Nancy and I slowly walked around the imposing courthouse building and past the attached parish jail, surrounded by razor wire, and then we parked ourselves on a set of stairs next to the courthouse and nervously waited for Laurie and Isaac, each of us lost in our own thoughts.

Laurie arrived first, pulling into the driveway in a bright red BMW. She hopped out and greeted us warmly, then told us that Isaac had just texted her and that he and his wife were on their way. Sure enough, just minutes later, Isaac and Denise appeared around the corner of the garage. He was well built, while she was petite and attractive. But despite his imposing physique, his expression was open, his eyes kind. My response to his presence surprised even me. Earlier in the day, while exercising in the hotel gym, I had been overcome by emotion—a mixture of sadness, grief, and gratitude all wrapped into one big cry. But when he turned that corner, with his wife protectively by his side, there were no tears—just relief.

We shook hands, but moments later, as we both stood in the doorway, I looked at him and said simply, "It's you," a throwback quote from *Sleepless in Seattle*. But what that statement captured for me was the simple fact that meeting him wasn't a big surprise, even as stunning as the whole thing was. Maybe my belief had been part of a delusional system that had helped me stay afloat all these years. I don't really know. But Isaac just seemed familiar.

We had gathered with no specific agenda other than to seek a deeper understanding of the events that had unfolded in the spring and fall of 1979, when a murder and a wrongful conviction devastated our two families and tethered our lives together forever. We took the elevator to Laurie's office, a place where things happened, where people's lives were changed in the most profound way. The animal-themed decorations—including a leopard-print carpet in the private elevator to her chambers and a vibrant red and blue dog painting—made it clear that Judge White loved animals, which I took as a good sign. During our time together I would also learn that she is an advocate of tough love, and that this tough love has saved many young men over the years—including Isaac. Nancy and I sat in separate chairs directly across from Isaac and his wife, who sat together on the couch. Laurie sat in the fulcrum position, to help mediate a conversation that seemed at the very least implausible.

And yet two hours later, we were still talking. In fact, we continued to talk for our entire three days in New Orleans.

One moment from that initial meeting captured the transformative power of this new connection. Isaac had already openly shared gut-wrenching stories about his arrest, the violent interrogation methods used by the detectives, and the hideous conditions of his first few days of incarceration in a building less than fifty feet from where we now sat. Denise asked what the murder had been like for our family. Nancy and I both began to share snippets of that horrible time, an event that neither of us have felt comfortable sharing with others. We talked about the confusion and pain surrounding our dad's murder, along with the character assassination of Isaac and the lies that were actively fed to our family as the prosecution fabricated a case against him. We had both been born and raised in Bangor, Maine, oblivious to the problems of large urban areas like New Orleans, where crime and violence were the backdrop of everyday life. Truth be told, I recalled my family taking comfort in the self-assured words of the detectives and prosecutors; we blindly trusted that they had our family's best interests at heart and, like us, only sought the truth about our father's murder. We needed the justice system to right the wrong that had been done to us. In fact, our sanity depended on it.

Isaac listened intently to both of us. I wasn't sure what to expect, but as a trauma therapist, I looked for the telltale signs of dissociation or even poor attention in Isaac, which would have been expected given the relentless brutality he had endured over the past three decades. But they weren't there, and when he spoke his words were a surprisingly soothing balm to our pain, which was still red hot and unapproachable. His words to Nancy were steady and filled with feeling: "I kept thinking of you when I was in prison—when I first got there, I already knew Dr. Banks had a young child. I wanted to reach out to you to see what I could do to help." My eyes filled with tears as I looked at my sister, who was eight years old at the time of the murder. She was gently weeping, and though she pinched the bridge of her nose with the fingers of her right hand in an unconscious effort to stem the flow of emotion, the tears rising from deep inside would not be stopped. Still, Isaac didn't look away, he didn't harden to the anguish or try to push it aside. He simply and directly asked, "Can I give you a hug?" As Isaac and Nancy embraced, the rest of us were in tears.

Isaac —

That first meeting in Laurie White's office was filled with uncertainty. However, when I was embraced by Amy and Nancy the skepticism soon dropped away. It took Denise a little longer in the meeting to drop her guard and accept the offer of friendship. But she did in the first meeting. When Nancy and I hugged, it was very powerful for me and I think for her too. It was such a beautiful experience being embraced by the daughters of the man I was wrongly imprisoned for killing. Amy was so nice; she is such an amazing person with a good spirit. Her smile, her way of talking, her tone—everything about her is positive. Though they asked for the meeting, it offered me a real sense of closure on that chapter of my life.

The meeting turned into more of a weekend. I felt obligated to protect Amy and Nancy from any harm while they were in New Orleans. Partly this was because I could imagine how bad it would look if something happened to them and people found out they were with me! But Denise and I genuinely enjoyed ourselves showing them around the city, teaching them about the wards and the damage that had been done during Katrina. And going back to Angola with Amy was very moving. When they were leaving it felt so good that the victim's family knew I was innocent. And their kindness speaks a lot about their dad—he definitely did a good job raising his children, he must have been a good man. We established a close bond that weekend and after they left, I missed them, I really missed them—that was so unexpected.

Amy —

Nancy and I asked Isaac if he had any records from the trial, and we were thrilled to hear that he had the trial transcript and the infamous Dillman Report. We couldn't wait to get our hands on them, and we made plans to meet with him the next day at the courthouse to pick up the legal documents along with a copy of an autobiographical manuscript that Isaac had written in federal prison.

From the courthouse the next morning, Isaac and Denise drove us to a Kinko's on the other side of town. In one of many surreal moments, the four of us went to work sorting, copying, and collating hundreds of pages of documents. As I watched Isaac—his reading glasses perched on the end of his nose as he focused on placing the copied documents back in order—I was struck by how easy it was to be with him. In the fantasy I had created about our meeting, there was no conversation, no laughter, just a frozen stare. I was entirely unprepared for how rich and resonant our connection felt from the start.

When the copying was done, Isaac and Denise took us on a tour of New Orleans, including the Ninth Ward, which had been decimated by Katrina; some of the neighborhoods that were home to his friends and family; and finally, Isaac's gym. This was where he now boxed and coached young children in the sport. It was immediately clear that in this small corner building, Isaac was king. The smell of sweat and leather hung in the air, and Isaac beamed with pride. I realized anew that this was a huge part of what had been stolen from him when he was wrongfully convicted of killing my father. It was the simple pleasure of being in the one place in the world where you knew you belonged. Of the many things that I was learning about Isaac, this one stood out front and center: Isaac was, and is, a boxer. It's in his bones and his blood.

The four of us weren't quite ready to part, so we stopped for lunch at the Ruby Slipper, the spot where Nancy and I had dined the day before. Over chicken dumplings, Isaac shared more stories of the horrors he faced in prison. Denise spoke of Isaac's transition back into mainstream society, how he had difficulty with crowds, and how she struggled to integrate him into her life after seventeen years without him. These were stressors that I couldn't even fathom, and I was reminded that despite the devastating and tragic death of my father, Isaac's daily traumas had been so much worse. The separation from his wife and kids, the loss of the prime years of his boxing career, and the routine disrespect that he suffered twenty-four hours a day for almost twenty-nine years. Years that belonged not to him, but to the prison system. When I tried to put myself in his shoes, I felt as if I were being smothered; the rage grew so large in my chest that I thought I would explode. I wanted to hurt someone. And yet, I sat across from a man who felt genuinely kind, even gentle. I knew then that I had so much to learn.

Back in the hotel room, Nancy and I dove into the copied material, starting with the Dillman report, a thirty-page document that detailed the police investigation into our father's murder. I had visualized the murder scene a million times through the years, but those details had been imagined, undoubtedly an amalgam of TV crime scenes. However, these fantasies would now be replaced by the vivid, stark description of the crime scene on page six of the report.

> The victim was lying in a supine position approximately thirty feet from the hotel entrance. His head was facing in an uptown direction, approximately thirty feet from the curbing of Loyola Street. The lower portion of the body

was bent at the waist, with both legs extended, crossed at the ankles, and pointing in a lake direction. The victim's right arm was bent at the elbow, pointing in an uptown direction. The left arm outstretched from the torso, pointed in a downtown direction. The victim's head was lying in a large amount of clotted blood, indicating that some type of head wound had been suffered. The body was clad in gray pants, black shoes, white silk shirt, and a pink and gray checked sport coat.

A few sentences later the injury was described:

The victim suffered a single gunshot wound to the left eye with no apparent exit wound. From all indications the entrance wound was an apparent contact type, as the wound was surrounded with powder residue.

From this description it became clear that in the struggle the murderer was close enough to place the gun directly on my father's face before he pulled the trigger. Each new clarifying detail sank into my soul, leaving a new layer of horror. His pockets were emptied, the intimate contents recorded in a detached, cold list, as though my father were being dissected:

Left front pocket—One pill bottle containing one yellow pill

Right front pocket—one pipe and one book of matches

Left front pants pocket—two black combs, one hotel key to the Hyatt Regency hotel room 1725, one silver dime, and one penny

Right front pants pocket—one black plastic comb, and one nail clipper

Right rear pants pocket—one black leather wallet containing one twenty-dollar bill, one ten-dollar bill, five one-dollar bills and personal papers, credit cards, etc. in the name of the victim.

Left ring finger—one yellow metal ring containing a black stone.

As I read the list, I remember thinking that I had never seen my father comb his hair, not that he didn't do it. But how strange to have three black combs on his person when he died! The description also brought back deep memories of watching my father pull his brown and black pipe out of a pocket, fill it with tobacco, and then light it with a match, delicately protecting the flame with a cupped hand. He would coax the flame into the barrel of the pipe with three quick sucking inhalations followed by one deep breath. And the familiar scent of Half and Half pipe tobacco would fill the air. The memory filled me with pure, clear sadness.

According to the Dillman report, the primary witness to the shooting, Tony Williams, described the man who fought with my father as being Black, five feet, nine inches tall, with a slim build, wearing a white short-sleeve shirt, blue jeans, and, perhaps most notably, a white sailor's cap pulled over his forehead. A few pages later came the most damning evidence against the prosecution, the potentially exculpatory material that eventually led to Isaac's release:

> On Monday, April 23, 1979, Detective Dillman received an interoffice correspondence from Sgt. Robert Italiano of the First District, which reflected the following information:
>
> On Thursday, April 19, 1979, Police Officer Smucin of the First District was involved in the apprehension of two Black males who had perpetrated an armed robbery at Canal Street and Elks Place. During the apprehension a .22 caliber Clark revolver containing five live rounds and one spent cartridge was recovered...Sgt. Italiono [sic] felt the two subjects that were arrested fit the general description of the two wanted subjects in the murder of Ronald Banks and wished to bring this information to the attention of the investigating detective.

Three arrests were made in that armed robbery attempt: Ricky Mazique, Derek Robertson, and Samuel Washington. The physical descriptions included an observation that Samuel Washington was wearing a sailor's cap at the time of the armed robbery. Four days later, ballistic testing proved that the shot that killed my father came from the gun recovered from these three assailants. It had been one thing to read a summary of the wrongful-conviction allegations against Paddison from newspaper reports, but quite another to look at the actual police report and realize that it should have been used not only to free Isaac, but also to arrest the person who had actually murdered my father.

24

THE PROSECUTOR

Amy Banks

Not long after reviewing the damning Dillman report, David Paddison picked us up at the hotel. He pulled up in a large silver car and jumped out to greet us. The whiplash was disorienting. I wanted to hate him, to greet him with scorn and a slap on the face, but when he reached for my hand, he was protective and paternal, perfectly tugging on the part of me that desperately longed for a father. He had taken time out of his busy weekend schedule to pull together the trial material, drive thirty minutes from his home in Covington to pick us up, and find a place where we could sift through the material.

During the drive he told us that he had left the DA's office in 1983 and moved his law practice to Covington. He explained that during his tenure in the DA's office he prosecuted thirty murder cases, ten of which resulted in death sentences; three of those had been carried out. In his mind, the death penalty added finality to the process; as he put it, "Enough nonsense, for enough time." He felt that as an assistant DA, he had done a "damn good job."

We ended up in the lobby of a nearby luxury hotel, where he led us to a quiet, out-of-the-way table. He assured us that he remembered our family and the tragedy we had gone through very well. In fact, he told us that he had been extremely upset that Isaac Knapper had been released from Angola, that he was positive that Isaac had fired the gun that killed our father. As if to punctuate his belief, he told us that the minute Isaac was released from Angola he began to sell drugs and ended up going right back to prison. In fact, he was pretty sure that Isaac was still there.

Before digging into the material, he offered a primer on how the DA's office worked back then. It would have been protocol for Detective Dillman to contact the DA's office on the night of the shooting to let them know that a murder case was coming their way. Once informed, the clock would begin to tick: The prosecution team then had thirty days to indict someone for the crime.

He admitted that early in the process they relied less on the actual police record to get people before a grand jury, and that the discovery process and the collection and sharing of facts with the defense were handled rather loosely. In the Knapper case, he said he was very familiar with one of the defendant's lawyers, Robert Zibilich, because he had helped mentor him as an attorney. The two men had an unwritten agreement that if they ended up on opposite sides of a case, Paddison would put the case file he was working on at the end of his desk and Zibilich would come and look at it whenever he wanted.

As evidence that he had shared all information with the defense team, Paddison told us that Judge Frank Shea had always made the defense appear in front of him to see if they had everything they needed from the prosecution. Furthermore, he cited a court record in which Zibilich was quoted as saying he was satisfied with what he had as proof that Paddison hadn't withheld evidence. It apparently did not occur to Paddison that both could be true—that if Zibilich was unaware of the Dillman report then he was operating blindly. Zibilich relied on the fairness of the system and his trust that his fellow colleagues wouldn't knowingly withhold information from the defense team. He believed this not only because it was the law, but because it's exactly the thing that holds our entire justice system together.

As we turned to the details of the shooting, Paddison commented that "these guys were hopped, usually on drugs," and he told us that he believed that Knapper had an "extensive juvenile record." When I asked for specifics, he admitted that he didn't know the nature of those offenses, although interestingly, an abbreviated version of Paddison's exact three words—"extensive juv. rec."—were written on Isaac's arrest warrant. Paddison also emphasized that John Dillman had been a homicide detective for many years in the New Orleans area and had connections in the projects, and he added that the Guste Housing Project [where Isaac lived] was "the worst."

Having just spent a couple of hours reading the Dillman report and the trial transcript, Nancy and I had some very specific questions for Mr. Paddison. The first was how his team had determined that Knapper had committed the shooting. He explained that the only witness at the scene, Tony Williams, picked Knapper out of a picture of potential shooters. Earlier that day Isaac had told us that Tony was a very unstable person who wouldn't have been a believable witness, which is exactly why he wasn't called to testify. When we suggested this, Paddison responded simply that they "probably couldn't find him."

As we discussed details of the murder, Paddison described the physical appearance of the two defendants. In his memory, Leroy Williams was lanky and Knapper was huge. From the photo of Isaac's arrest, which had been seared into my brain so long ago, I knew that he wasn't a big teenager at the time of the murder. When I paused for clarification, Paddison simply told us that Knapper was a boxer who weighed in at about 220 pounds at the time of the murder. I dug through my papers and found a copy of the newspaper clipping showing Detective Dillman holding Isaac's cuffed hands behind his back. Isaac appears young and less muscular than Dillman—he couldn't have weighed more than 170, tops. When shown the evidence, Paddison backpedaled a bit, reframing his point by saying that "relative to the tall and lanky Williams, Knapper seemed like a large, well-built boy." He didn't seem to be bothered by the contradiction.

For Nancy and me, the fact that the murder weapon was found in the hands of three other boys a week later in another robbery seemed central to Knapper's innocence, so I asked him directly how he made sense of this piece of evidence. Again, his response was vague but definitive. "The weapon was juggled around by these guys." In fact, he believed that there was a discussion in the police report about the gun being stolen, although Nancy and I couldn't find any evidence of that.

As we pushed him a little on these questions he volunteered with a mild defensiveness that "Knapper never denied that he was there" and then wondered out loud why Knapper had never taken the stand in his own defense. He rhetorically asked what kind of person doesn't take the stand to defend himself when he's faced with the possibility of going to prison for the rest of his life. The statement made me pause, and I made a mental note to ask Isaac exactly that.

Paddison eventually ended the discussion by saying that "the whole case was Leroy Williams—Leroy Williams was a believable witness." He wrapped up the conversation as seamlessly as he had the one-day trial.

To be fair, Paddison did have some documents that we hadn't seen yet, but it grew increasingly clear that he had a strange paranoia about Laurie White—he even proposed that as a Catholic she had somehow managed to get the Catholic church involved in bringing him up on charges because, later in his career, he had been involved in some of the first cases of priest abuse of children. This explanation apparently helped him understand why Laurie and Isaac had pursued disciplinary action against him a decade and a half after the original trial, when the simpler explanation is that for twelve of those years, Isaac had been behind bars.

I left the meeting honestly grateful that Paddison had agreed to share what he remembered, and I was appreciative of his warmth, but I still never got the feeling that afternoon—not once—that he knew Isaac Knapper was a human being. And of course, this is almost certainly how the whole mess happened in the first place.

After another large dinner and another bottle of Prosecco, Nancy and I retired to our hotel room to reflect on the day and read more of the material we had gathered from Isaac. We were both stunned to find pages and pages of court transcripts in which the prosecution team was indeed questioning Knapper on the witness stand. And not only did Isaac take the stand, he clearly and repeatedly defended himself against the charges of murder, even as Paddison's partner, Foret, became more and more aggressive and condescending. It didn't seem to me that this was something a man defending himself against an accusation of unethical practice could easily forget. It made me feel deeply, deeply sick.

25

FAMILY

Amy Banks

To prepare for our trip to Angola, I read everything I could about the prison and watched the Netflix reality TV show *Louisiana Lockdown,* which was taped at Angola. These sources gave me a distant, disconnected sense of the prison's structure and atmosphere, no more than a superficial sense of what to expect: darkness and despair.

After breakfast the next morning Nancy and I walked back to the courthouse, where we joined a small group of people heading to the prison. Laurie had invited us over the summer—she wanted us to get a firsthand look at the successful prison-reform program that she and Arthur Hunter had started to rehabilitate young first offenders who had been incarcerated for certain low-level crimes. At sentencing, a prisoner may be selected to enter the reform program at Angola, where his release is predicated on his completion of two certificate programs in basic technological skills such as welding, auto mechanics, and HVAC. During their time in prison, the new inmates are paired up with lifers who teach them these skills and act as their mentors; they're designed to be living reminders of the path that should be avoided at all costs. This is the ultimate win-win scenario for the prison: The lifers get a sense of meaning and purpose that helps them cope with the fact that they're never going to leave prison, while the newly convicted men are able to learn a trade and some life lessons, both of which could ultimately prevent them from returning to Angola for the rest of their lives.

After he serves two years of his sentence, provided he has a certain level of structure awaiting him outside, the inmate is released. He must join a religious community, find a home to live in, and secure a job. It's not easy, but those who complete the program leave with a real chance to get off the streets, get off drugs, and start a life for themselves that will give them the ability to earn both respect and money to support their families.

The program is supported by funds raised by the famous Angola Rodeo, which has been held at the prison since 1965. Originally a source of distraction and entertainment for inmates and staff, the event has grown into one of the most well-attended prison rodeos in the country; it is now held twice a year at the prison's rodeo center, which was built in 2000.

In addition to meeting on a regular basis with each of the inmates in the reform program—either on Skype or in person in her courtroom—Laurie also visits Angola a couple of times a year to give pep talks to the program participants. For this trip, a few other people who were active in prison reform joined us; one woman had spent time in prison and was now involved in prison-reform programs with a personal intensity and passion.

As the rest of the group dispersed into various vehicles for the trip (Isaac and Denise rode in their own car), Nancy and I walked with Laurie to her black Mercedes. After opening the door, she casually threw a gun into the console between the driver and passenger seat; I made a mental note that this was the area in my car usually reserved for gum and lip balm. "Y'all don't mind the gun, do you?" she asked. Nancy and I looked at each other, wide-eyed, having just had a quick lesson in cultural differences. "You gals are Yankees—you don't do guns up there. I don't go anywhere without mine." And off we went, to the bloodiest prison in America.

The drive was long, 130 miles northwest from New Orleans. The last twenty miles took us over Louisiana State Highway 66, a winding, completely isolated rural road. Laurie was a comfortable conversationalist: direct, honest, and occasionally harsh in her opinions and judgments. Nancy and I were all ears and had dozens of questions; like kids in a candy shop, we were starving for information, sure that even the most mundane facts could help sort out the puzzle of pain in our lives. She shared snippets of Isaac's life after his release from Angola at age twenty-nine. How he had struggled to work for other people, not surprisingly intolerant and distrustful of authority figures. How he had fallen in love with two women and ended up with two families to support. How he had turned to drug dealing when his boxing career began to flounder, but had told Denise he was running a successful liquor store. And how, more than anything else, Isaac was all about his kids. She spoke about him much like a big sister would of an adored younger brother who keeps messing up his life and turning to her for help. They seemed tied together by a bond more mysterious than love and larger than family. It's hard to fathom this connection, which was built around the simple fact that she saved his life.

As we approached Baton Rouge, Laurie switched gears and told us we were going to pick up her brother, who had suffered a serious head injury when he was fourteen but was now living independently. This provided an opening into Laurie's family. She grew up in Baton Rouge, the youngest of three children. She announced with legal clarity, "I had a crazy mother and a crazy sister. Really, my mother was very odd." She said her mother was narcissistic, and she confessed that her own first marriage had failed because she had "married my mother." She described her parents as Southerners with a subpar education, and she told us that she was the only one of her siblings to get a college degree.

Her father, she explained, was a "commuting farmer," a term for someone who traveled to other farms to work. She and her siblings attended public schools, and she decided in the third grade to become a lawyer simply because her initials spelled "LAW." It was a sign, she told us. She attended law school at LSU and set up practice in New Roads, Louisiana.

We arrived at her brother's house, and he slid into the seat next to Nancy. He was pleasant and conversant, and a slight youthfulness was the only evidence of the distant head injury.

For the last hour of our ride Laurie told us more about the prison-reform program, which won an ACA award in 2014 for "innovative prison action."

The twenty-mile dirt road to Angola has now been partially paved, which helped speed up the last leg of the drive. There isn't much along the road—renamed the Tunica Trace Byway in 1988—other than a few crossing routes that end in small rural communities. As the prison came into view in the distance, I felt a heaviness settle over me. The atmosphere in the car seemed to thicken with tension and anticipation as we approached the prison gates, even though the entrance could easily be mistaken for a highway tollbooth—that is, if one ignored the large brick sign to the right of the gate that announced "The Louisiana State Penitentiary," along with the intimidating barbed-wire fences that marked the prison boundaries.

Laurie pulled into a small parking lot and waited for the rest of our caravan. After security checks were done, we were invited to tour the prison museum, which is filled with images and artifacts of the prison's long, rich, and horrendous history. One wall is taken up with a life-size image of the execution table, while another bears the weight of a large cabinet filled with handmade weapons confiscated from inmates over the years. A third wall features a stunning image of an inmate dressed in black tails and top hat sitting at the reins of a vintage black hearse pulled by two large white Percheron horses. From my readings, I knew that the hearse was carrying the unclaimed body of an inmate to Point Lookout, the prison cemetery.

The prison shop, meanwhile, offered a selection of mugs, T-shirts, and bumper stickers adorned with such slogans as "Angola—A Gated Community," and Nancy and I spent a few uncomfortable moments debating the merits of buying prison merchandise. But after hearing that all proceeds go to prison programs that benefit the inmates, we each bought a stack of gifts for friends and relatives. And then we all piled into a large white prison van for a tour of the grounds.

Riding through Angola prison with Isaac was perhaps the

most surreal experience of our entire trip. He pointed out the "sights" along the way: death row and its long, narrow, caged walking area, through which condemned inmates are allowed to walk one at a time for forty-five minutes a day; "the hole," in which he spent months and even years in solitary confinement; and the fields where the inmates plant and harvest most of the food they eat. At one point the van stopped at a large repair shop manned by inmates, most of whom would never leave Angola. These lifers had spent decades building up their reputation in the prison until they gained "trustee" status, which gave them more freedoms and privileges than the other men. The trustees are a central part of the prison-reform program. Though they will never leave Angola, their role as teachers and mentors to the younger inmates helps provide them with a community and a purpose in life.

At one stop we entered a large building in which inmates learned HVAC repair and maintenance. A large group of men (almost exclusively men of color) had gathered to hear Laurie speak. She walked to the front of the room, clearly comfortable talking with these young men. Her pep talk included tips on discipline and reminders of what was expected of them in the reform program. It was strange to see this white, middle-aged woman engaging these young men, but engage them she did. She introduced Isaac as a powerful example of what not to do—that is, not to blow a second chance by selling drugs or returning to other criminal activity. And then Isaac spoke, sharing snippets of his life experience at Angola.

Laurie then spontaneously introduced Nancy and me to the group— first name only—and explained that our father had been murdered on the streets of New Orleans in a robbery. Eyes briefly turned to us with some curiosity, and in that moment I locked eyes with a young man in the front row. I couldn't imagine what he must have been thinking, but his stare was intense and slightly unnerving. After the gathering we climbed back into the van and drove to lunch in the warden's dining area.

At each stop of the tour, Isaac greeted old friends and was met with fondness and respect. He had called ahead to the warden's office to see if an old friend, Michael, could join the group for lunch. Michael had been in Angola for more than thirty years, and decades of good behavior had earned him trustee status. As we sat at a long table, an older gentleman dressed in typical inmate attire—blue jeans and a white T-shirt—entered the house. Isaac jumped up and greeted him with a warm, tight embrace. This was Michael.

Isaac had stressed to us his certainty that Michael had been convicted of a crime he hadn't committed, and as I looked across the table at Michael, I realized I had never seen such sad, hollow eyes. His gentle demeanor was hard to read. Was this his true spirit I was seeing, or was he simply a man so broken by the system that he had no fight left? Isaac was like a happy puppy beside him, thrilled to see his old friend, and while Michael welcomed the engagement, he also commented that there was no longer anything for him to leave prison for; every important person in his life had died while he was inside. Seeing Michael was completely heartbreaking, and I suspect that his worn face will leave a lasting impression on me.

Lunch was prepared and served by a towering inmate whose appeal for early parole had been recently rejected; he was settling in for another long spell of hopelessness while lawyers filed a new appeal of his life sentence. That's when the obvious fact that not everyone in Angola has been wrongly convicted struck me. Many men have raped and murdered, some more than once. At the same time, many of those men have served more than a decade of their life sentences with no problems. They're essentially rehabilitated, but their life sentences offer little potential for release. These men live in bipolar swells of hope and despair. After each defeat of an appeal or denial of parole, they must adjust their expectations to the confines of prison life, or risk their sanity.

After lunch, we loaded back into the van and traveled to the center of the prison, where inmates were building two chapels within a stone's throw of each other. As we walked down a long hallway, Isaac looked a little shaken. He pointed to a cement building a hundred yards to his right and said simply, "This is where I was put first when I got here." He was physically reliving the moment when his life was hijacked as a sixteen-year-old boy and he was thrown into a violent prison system, complete with a huge, crazy cellmate. His fear, not surprisingly, was palpable—a reminder of how deeply traumatizing his life had been in this murderous environment.

As we moved into the second chapel we stumbled upon two convicts standing at the altar singing a stunning aria that pierced my heart with its beauty. Its tone seemed to capture the human spirit's ability to soar above any confinement. As I stood listening, I started to cry, and Denise moved closer and touched me in a simple, welcome act of comfort.

When the tour ended, Denise and Isaac offered to drive Nancy and me to the airport for our flight back to New York. During the two-hour trip, we talked nonstop with Isaac, sharing one story after another. Every one of his ended with a friend or a family member dead. His stories weren't designed to elicit sympathy or concern from us; he was simply sharing the facts of his life. As I listened it dawned on me that it was nothing short of a miracle that he was still alive, and I was filled with gratitude that I had been able to meet him in person. I didn't yet know how my life would change or how I might grow from this experience, but I was aware of how seminal it felt, and what a gift it already was.

Isaac finally pulled his Lexus up to the curb outside the airport, then helped us carry our bags into the terminal. I was surprised by the emotion I felt, by the connection to this man who had been in my life for some thirty-six years. It seemed impossible to let go, to move forward with no clear plan for how to maintain the connection, unsure of what the impact had been on him but knowing clearly that this had changed me, that it had healed me at the very center of my being. We hugged once, twice, three times, and when we finally parted I could see in his eyes that he, too, was having a hard time saying goodbye. As a parting gift he said simply, "It feels like I'm saying goodbye to family." And at that moment I knew that we'd be okay, that we wouldn't lose each other, because we had both lost so much already in ways over which we had no control.

Family. It's such a simple word that describes a built-in sense of belonging. Some families you're born into; others you choose; and still others, in rare cases, you're thrust into. Our lives, so disparate in every way, blew up together on April 12, 1979. And in many ways, we've all been spiraling out of control, fighting to steady ourselves against the power of that explosion. And finally, through the years, through the pain, through the losses, as our lives whirled by each other's, we reached out a hand, touched each other, and simply held on.

ACKNOWLEDGEMENTS

Many people helped Isaac and me along our journey. First and foremost, our editor, Jaynie Royal and the team at Regal House Publishing and Pact Press who saw the potential in our story. Your guidance brought the story together more coherently and with more clarity than we could have imagined. Your editing suggestions allowed our story to develop into the book it wanted to be. A deep, deep thank you for the support and care.

A huge thank you to Gary Perkinson who discovered the story of Isaac's exoneration and generously copy edited our original manuscript and to Beth McGilley who read and offered feedback on every written word when the book was in its infancy. Your direction, help and support were instrumental. Likewise, Kate Banks read an early version of the manuscript and offered invaluable input on the structure and content of the book.

Thank you also to Katheryn Flynn who offered early support when the book was just an idea and helped shape the formal book proposal. A special appreciation to Jayme Banks who suggested the perfect title—*Fighting Time*.

Amy Banks
On a personal note, in the early years after my father's murder, many people supported me and my family—Shelly Gavitt, Cyndee Stacy, Julie Treadwell, Linda Clohosey, Doug Farnham, Kyle Kirkland. More recently, Sheryl Rosner, Martha Pavlakis, Angel Seibring, Lisa Langhammer and Karen Craddock have listened patiently and offered support in my journey over the past few years. Your friendship is felt deeply.

My colleagues at the Jean Baker Miller Training Institute and the International Center for Growth in Connection (Maureen Walker, Judith Jordan, Harriet Schwartz and Myriam Barenbaum) have been a steady reminder of the transformative power of relationships and the importance of social justice. Their courage and clarity have helped me walk the walk. My therapist of almost thirty years, Cynthia Kettyle, has been a rock in my life, helping me to find and name the frozen feelings locked away all of these years. Words cannot adequately express my gratitude for the stability and sanity you have brought to my life.

A special thank you to Judith Jordan and Melissa Coco who read final copies of the book and offered loving feedback to help me deal with the anticipation of the emotional exposure the book would bring. Judge Laurie White was instrumental in bringing this book to print—first by securing Isaac's release from Angola in 1992 and then by facilitating contact between Isaac and me. Thank you for your generous response to my requests and for being an ally of the relationship we have built.

To Isaac and Denise and their extended family—thank you for opening your hearts and your minds to my request to meet. Your warmth, love and decency in the face of the injustice you have been subjected too is stunning and your pain touches me deeply. Our relationship is the silver lining to this entire process.

To my family of origin, Kate, Phil, Nancy and my mom, Helena Banks—I have such deep love and admiration for the ways we have all tried to move forward. To Jayme, Alex and Judy—thank you for loving me despite my woundedness and for making life fun and meaningful. Watching my children grow up to become caring and kind human beings has healed my soul.

And finally, thank you to my sister and best friend, Nancy, who has been by my side on many adventures—but none bigger than this one! I could not have done it with anyone else. Love you.

Isaac Knapper

To my children, Raquel, Sasha, Isaac III, Ivory and Isis—who have always given me hope, inspiration and motivation. Love you with every breath.

To my wife, Denise Knapper whose kindness never waivers, respect never falters, and love never changes. To my brother, Corneal and my sisters, Hazel, Linda, Maxine, Christine and Betty—love you all.

To my lawyer and good friend, Judge Laurie White—thank you for always believing in me and thank you for your friendship and love. To my friend, Tom Wilson—thank you for having my back and giving me a shoulder to lean on. To my nephews and nieces, aunties and uncles—love to you all.

To my friends and comrades, Joe Louis, Albert Woodfox and Michael Johnson—a deep thank you.

And to the two ladies I am about to acknowledge—they are two of the most amazing people I have ever met. They're warm, thoughtful, and courageous and it gives me exquisite satisfaction to acknowledge these two wonderful people as my friends—Amy and Nancy Banks.

Last but not least, my mother, Clara Lee James, the heart of my soul and the love of my life. I love you mom.

JUSTICE REFORM RESOURCES

While *Fighting Time* is a deeply personal story to Amy and Isaac, it is also an all too familiar story about systemic racism in the U.S. Criminal Justice System. To learn more about mass incarceration, the school-to prison pipeline, wrongful conviction and other issues related to systemic racism in the justice system we offer the following resources:

The Equal Justice Initiative – The Equal Justice Initiative is committed to ending mass incarceration and excessive punishment in the United States, to challenging racial and economic injustice, and to protecting basic human rights for the most vulnerable people in American society.
https://eji.org

The Innocence Project - founded in 1992 by Peter Neufeld and Barry Scheck at Cardozo School of Law, exonerates the wrongly convicted through DNA testing and reforms the criminal justice system to prevent future injustice.
https://innocenceproject.org

Healing Justice - a national nonprofit organization that serves individuals who have experienced trauma and inequity in our justice system. Through restorative justice and justice reform, we provide post-trial support and recovery to crime victims, survivors, and their families. We also provide post-prison support and recovery to returning citizens and their families in cases where innocence has been proven.
https://healingjusticeproject.org

Nation Inside – a platform that connects and supports people who are building a movement to systematically challenge mass incarceration in the United States.
https://nationinside.org

Color of Change - helps people respond effectively to injustice in the world around us. As a national online force driven by 7 million members, we move decision makers in corporations and government to create a more human and less hostile world for Black people, and all people. Until justice is real.

https://colorofchange.org

JustLeadershipUSA – led by people directly impacted by the inequities in the social justice system, JustLeadershipUSA is dedicated to decarcerating the United States by educating, elevating and empowering the people and communities most impacted by systemic racism to drive meaningful and lasting policy reform

https://jlusa.org

Families Against Mandatory Minimums - FAMM's greatest asset has always been the stories of its members. By sharing the impact of unjust sentencing and prison policies on incarcerated individuals, their families, and their communities, FAMM has helped create urgency around the issue and made the problem feel real to the policymakers who have to be moved to make meaningful change. This two-pronged approach — public education and targeted advocacy — is core to FAMM's success to date and will remain critical to its work as the organization expands its organizing efforts nationally.

https://famm.org

National Juvenile Justice Network - Through education, community-building and leadership development, the National Juvenile Justice Network enhances the capacity of juvenile justice coalitions and organizations in 44 states and the District of Columbia to press for state and federal laws, policies and practices that are fair, equitable and developmentally appropriate for all children, youth and families involved in, or at risk of becoming involved in, the justice system.

https://www.njjn.org